PORTRAITS

OF

EMINENT AMERICANS

NOW LIVING;

WITH

BIOGRAPHICAL AND HISTORICAL MEMOIRS OF THEIR LIVES AND ACTIONS.

LIVINGSTON,

E NEW YORK BAR.

THIS PART CONTAINS

PRESIDENT PIERCE AND HIS CABINET;

WITH

GRIER, AND CATRON, OF THE U. S. SUPREME COURTS.

VOLUME IV.

TERMS OF THE WORK, SEE CIRCULAR PRECEDING THIS PART.

New York:
157 BROADWAY.
London:
SAMPSON LOW, SON & CO.
Paris:
A. & W. GALIGNANI & CO.

1854.

Price of this Part, One Dollar.

☞ *Terms, three dollars a year, in advance: those not willing to subscribe, will please remit twenty-five cents for this number.*

LIVINGSTON'S MONTHLY LAW MAGAZINE FOR 1854.

THAT the merit of this periodical may become more extensively known, we send to many of our friends, as a specimen for their examination, the January number. Such only as shall remit the subscription for the year will be considered subscribers; none others will receive any succeeding issue. Those who are not willing to subscribe, *will please remit twenty-five cents as the price of this number alone.* It *need not* be returned to the publisher.

The work should receive universal patronage, because each monthly number contains legal information which every lawyer should have at his command—while our reasonable terms, and the present low rates of postage, place it within the reach of all; rendering it, in fact, the cheapest, and best work in this country for the practicing lawyer.

Every line of the "Monthly Law Magazine" shall be devoted to matter useful to the practicing lawyer. It will continue to furnish excellent steel portraits of eminent lawyers, but no biographical sketch of more than one or two pages in length will accompany the likenesses. Long articles, or disquisitions on subjects more abstruse and curious than useful, will be omitted; for, however interesting these might prove to the cloistered scholar, they are, generally, mere accumulations of learning, of little practical value, and not to be turned to account in the business of life. Our pages are too precious to be wasted upon speculative questions, which might be left to the combined wisdom of some debating society or Pickwick Club. Interminable disputations upon mere airy nothings and impalpable inanities will not find a place in this periodical. We trust it will keep up with the practical character of the present age, the fruits of which are seen, as well in the reform of the errors and absurdities of laws and customs of the middle ages, as in those wonderful inventions and powers which enrich human life, and dispense the blessings of Providence over every region. Though the Law Magazine will frequently contain original articles of value, by far its most *important feature* will be the *condensed reports of the latest cases;* for by giving these, we hope to render the work indispensable to every lawyer who has, or expects to have, a cause on the calendar. Many of the most important cases, of very general application and influence, involving either new principles of general interest, or the novel application of those already established, are passing under the careful observation and discriminating judgment of the several state courts, which are presided over by men of talents, learning, and profound sagacity. But the regular volumes of reports for the several states are too expensive to be purchased by many, and far too bulky and numerous to be read by those who can afford to pay for them. In many of these volumes, too, there are an accumulation of cases more or less deficient in establishing any great or new principle; the reporters seeming to publish, not so much on the principle of rejecting all which do not contain a *great deal*, as of adopting all that contain any thing The first object of this Magazine will be to place within the reach of all, condensed reports of the leading cases of general interest decided in the American and English courts. Such arrangements have been perfected with the prominent judges of every state to furnish manuscript decisions, and with reporters to supply early sheets, as warrants our saying that we shall be able to give subscribers *the earliest information of all leading cases.* Our reports will be placed in their hands several months before the same can appear in the regular reporters' volumes. These condensed reports have been, and are intended to be, of a much higher order than a mere abridgment; *the matter will not be abbreviated so as to omit any thing that is important, or which in any manner forms an essential feature of the case.* In every case, such a statement of the facts of the cause shall be made, as will fully and accurately exemplify the decision; and in the most important cases, the whole opinion delivered by the court will be given in the language of the court.

There is scarcely a practicing lawyer in the land who has not, at times, when hurried in the preparation of causes, fretted at having to wade through whole pages of barren, profitless verbosity, before he can get at the gist of the matter, which, after all, may lay in a nut-shell. Again, there is nothing of which he can more justly complain, than the frequency of *dicta* upon points not directly presented on the record, and which, while they throw no light on the particular case, do not

[*Continued on third page of cover.*

CIRCULAR.

INFORMATION RELATIVE TO THE GREAT WORK NOW PUBLISHING, CALLED

PORTRAITS AND MEMOIRS

OF

EMINENT AMERICANS NOW LIVING.

EMBRACING THE PLAN OF PUBLICATION AND ITS DESIGN, REMARKS CONCERNING ENGRAVING AND BIOGRAPHY, WITH NOTICES OF THE PRESS, THE CONTENTS OF THE NEW VOLUME, ETC., ETC.

BY JOHN LIVINGSTON, OF THE NEW YORK BAR.

PLAN OF PUBLICATION.

THIS work is issued in Parts, at the price of one dollar each. Every Part contains at least ten portraits and sketches, and is complete in itself. Five parts make a volume. Four volumes of about five hundred pages each, and containing at least fifty fine steel portraits and memoirs, have been already published. Every volume is a complete work in itself, so that any one can be purchased separately by such as do not desire the whole series. The four volumes contain 208 portraits, with biographical sketches of the first men of the United States now living, including President Pierce and every member of his cabinet, justices of the supreme court of the United States, governors of the various states, prominent army officers, lawyers, merchants, bankers, etc., as well as those of other vocations, from every section of the Union. The portraits in the four volumes just completed have been made at an expense of over twenty thousand dollars, and are among the finest specimens of artistic skill. The fifth volume is now in course of publication. The work, so far as already published, or any volume desired, will be sent to any part of the United States on receipt of the price, which is five dollars a volume. Being a work of very expensive character, it is published almost exclusively by subscription, and the best way to obtain it is to send direct to the publisher, by mail, and on receipt of the money he will forward the work to any part of the United States.

Money, either in gold or solvent bills, may be safely sent by mail, to John Livingston, 157 Broadway, New York, to whom all communications in regard to the publication must be addressed.

PLAN AND DESIGN OF THE WORK.

It presents to the world sketches, with pen and pencil, of some of those prominent Americans now living—including clergymen, lawyers doctors, soldiers, statesmen, financiers, merchants, manufacturers, and those of all other respectable vocations—whose talents, energy, and enterprise, while affording an instructive lesson to mankind, seem worthy of being held up as examples for emulation. That the memory of such persons should have its public record is peculiarly proper, because a knowledge of men whose substantial fame rests upon their attainments, character, and success must exert a wholesome influence on the rising generation of the American people; while to those who have arrived at a period in life not to be benefited by lessons designed for less advanced age, it can not fail to prove interesting.

While transmitting to posterity the memory of distinguished persons of the present day, it will instill in the minds of our children the important lesson, that honor and station are the sure reward of continued exertion—and that, compared to a good education, with habits of honest industry and economy, the greatest fortune would be but a poor inheritance. If it contains the memoirs of many who have enjoyed every advantage which affluence and early education can bestow, it also traces the history of those who, by their own unaided efforts, have risen from obscurity to the highest and most responsible trusts in the land.

The engravings preserve all the spirit and originality of their subjects, and are distinguished not only by their boldness and clearness of tone, but by the true artistic feeling that pervades them. In the choice of position, graceful arrangement, and the various other incidents which go to make the *ensemble* of a pleasing and effective picture, they are unrivaled. The portraits in this great work form, perhaps, the most complete and valuable collection in existence in this country. Taken from life, they present to us an exact reproduction of the familiar traits of men whose deeds live enshrined in our hearts. To the present generation their value is great, but to the next it will be immense. What would we not give to look upon the images, thus reproduced, of Washington, Jefferson, Patrick Henry? By continuing to devote itself to the task of illustrating the men who illustrate the country, this work will perpetuate the fame it has already acquired.

It is useless to expatiate on the uses and charms of the art of engraving, for which this work has done so much; indeed, it is not too much to say that it has paid more to engravers than any other enterprise in this country. The art of engraving is so intimately connected with the elegant literature, the general cultivation, and even the amusements of our times, that even those who have no practical skill in it know and feel much of the extent of its majesty and power. Like painting, it is a natural and universal language, the language of description through the eye, in its elements common to all mankind; through the senses awakening the imagination, and by her aid reanimating the dead. It is an art which appeals directly to the patronage, the judgment, and the natural affections of all, and ministers to the best feelings of the human heart. It rescues from oblivion the once-loved features of the absent or the dead; it is the memorial of filial or parental affection; it perpetuates the presence of the mild virtue, the heartfelt kindness, the humble piety which, in other days, filled our affections and cheered our lives. In the hour of affliction and bereavement, to use the words of a living poet,

"Then for a beam of joy to light
  In memory's sad and wakeful eye,
Or banish from the noon of night
  Her dreams of deeper agony.

Shall song its witching cadence roll,
  Yea, even the tenderest airs repeat,
Which breath'd when soul was knit to soul,
  And heart to heart responsive beat?

What visions wake—to charm—to melt!
  The lov'd, the lost, the dead are near:
Oh, hush that strain, too deeply felt,
  And cease that solace too severe.

But thou, serene and silent Art,
  By Heaven's own light wer't taught to lend
A milder solace to the heart,
  The sacred image of a Friend.

No specter forms of pleasure fled,
  Thy soft'ning, sweet'ning tints restore,
For thou can give us back the dead,
  Ev'n in the loveliest looks they wore."

It is an exalted and sacred office which Art discharges, when it can thus administer to the charities of domestic life. But engraving becomes public and national when—as in this work—it is employed in perpetuating the expression of the mind speaking in the features of the brave, the good, the great—of those whose valor has won our battles, or by whose wisdom we may become wise—of the heroes of our own country—of the patriots of our own history—of the men of business and humanity—of the benefactors of the human race. Then it becomes, indeed, a teacher of morality, it then assists in the education of youth, giving form and life to their abstract perceptions of duty and excellence. The young man who examines and studies this work must be dull and brutal indeed if he is not roused into aspirations after excellence—if the countenances of the men who look upon him do not sometimes fill his soul with generous thoughts and high contemplations.

Why should we not have everywhere these incitements to laudable exertion and honorable ambition? We should spread abroad, over our whole land, this mixed and mighty influence,

> "Of the morals of the arts,
> Which mould a people's hearts."

We have great men to honor, and talent enough to do honor to them. In our public libraries, in our courts of justice, our legislative halls, and seminaries of education, the eye should everywhere meet memorials of worth.

Engraving stands in the same relation to the daguerreian art and portrait painting that printing does to eloquence and poetry; it brings the productions of both within the reach of many thousands to whom they would otherwise have been wholly inaccessible. It enables every one to bring the great actors of the present day within our own doors—to make them, as it were, spectators of the blessings they have earned for us, and to place them before the eyes of our children.

The relatives of the subjects of this splendid enterprise should feel grateful for what it has done. True, it does not portray the features, relate the history, and perpetuate the virtuous deeds of its subjects in a statuary of brass and marble, as did the Athenian republic in ancient times; but it accomplishes the same great object in equally as imperishable a form, and one far more useful and instructive. Modern science has enabled it to accomplish in a few weeks what but a short time ago years of toil could not have produced. Through that wonderful discovery, whereby the light of heaven is made the artist, one minute can complete a more faithful likeness than was ever wrought by painter's pencil. The labor of a month enables the engraver to transfer to a steel plate this sun-developed portrait, with its finest lights, shadows, and tints: and thus the work is done whereby the likeness may be multiplied to the number of hundreds of thousands. A steel engraving will print *one thousand* portraits a day, each one of which mav be of more value than the finest painting. No one to whom the opptunity is presented of thus forever preserving his features, should fail to embrace it. If we will but reflect upon the marked mortality among those with whom we have been most intimately acquainted, and how greatly we should value their images, were they in our possession, we shall be able to conceive how important it is that an accurate delineation of our features should be obtained, as well for the gratification of friends now living as of those who may come after us.

It is needless to remark on the extended information and delight we derive from the multiplication of portraits by engraving, or on the more important advantages resulting from the study of biography. Separately considered, the one affords an amusement not less innocent than elegant, inculcates the rudiments, or aids the progress of taste, and rescues from the hand of time the perishable monuments raised by the pencil or the daguerreian art. The other—while it is, perhaps, the more agreeable branch of historical literature—is certainly the more useful in its moral effects; stating the known circumstances, and endeavoring to unfold the secret motives of human conduct; selecting all that is worthy of being recorded; bestowing its lasting encomiums and chastisements, it at once informs and invigorates the mind, warms and mends the heart. It is, however, from the combination of portrait and biography that we reap the utmost degree of utility and pleasure which can be derived from them. As, in contemplating the portrait of an eminent person, we long to be instructed in his history, so, in considering his actions, we are anxious to behold his countenance. So earnest is this desire, that the imagination is generally ready to coin a set of features or to conceive a character to supply the painful absence of one or the other. It is impossible to conceive a work which ought to be more interesting than one which will exhibit before our progeny their fathers as they lived, accompanied with such memoirs of their lives and characters as shall furnish a comparison of persons and countenances with sentiments and actions.

The memoirs are accurate and authentic, recourse having been invariably had to the most competent and unequivocal authorities in the statement of facts. Each sketch is accompanied by an exact and well-executed portrait of its subject, engraved in the best manner on steel, from daguerreotypes, expressly for the work. Some of the first talent in the country has been employed on the engravings; and no effort has been wanting to render the work splendid as well as valuable—one which will equally adorn the library or embellish the parlor.

The work is handsomely gotten up, and admirably sustained. No enterprise of the kind can hold out greater inducements for the exercise of the best energies of the people, and the moral and patriotic devotion which adorns our nature, than the promise that the enterprising, talented, and honorable citizen, whatsoever may be his profession or occupation, shall find at least the reward due to his labors and his virtues in the knowledge and affection of his countrymen.

While preserving the memory and perpetuating the living images of some of the great and good of this generation, this work will also place before the public examples begetting an emulation which must kindle that honorable ambition forming the main incentive to vigorous exertion and great and noble actions. And if, in but a single instance, the record of one of these lives, from obscurity up through the arduous paths of manhood to distinction, shall kindle laudable ambition, invigorate patriotic resolves, or cheer afresh the struggling aspirant to renewed and incessant endeavors, the author will feel that his labors have not been unrewarded.

REMARKS CONCERNING BIOGRAPHY.

It is a duty which every man owes to society to aid in furnishing such facts as may be necessary to enable the biographer to prepare his memoir; in no case can there be any objection to the practice, for it has been supported both by precedent and by the highest authority of ancient and modern times.

Tacitus says, to transmit to posterity the lives and characters of men of consideration was an office frequently performed in ancient times. Many, from the remotest period, have even been their own historians, persuaded that in speaking of themselves they should display an honest confidence in their integrity; and it will be remembered Rutilius and Scaurus left an account of their own lives, the truth of which has never been doubted. Even Cicero himself, in his letter to his friend Lucceius, acknowledges his ambition to live in history, and avows his hopes of obtaining from the remembrance of after ages a glorious immortality, as well as the pleasure of enjoying his posthumous fame in his own lifetime, and intimates his intention of following the example of many illustrious men who had written their own history.

Biography is that branch of history that relates exclusively to man, and embraces within its limits all that appertains to his moral, intellectual, social, or professional character; in other words, the discharge of his relative duties to this world, and his higher obligations to the world to come. Thus considered, while it is true that "history is philosophy teaching by example," the sentiment is more especially applicable to biography, which is one of the chief elements of history.

The life and progress of man, his virtues and his vices, his accomplishments and defects, his successes and misfortunes, his triumphs and defeats, his motives and his actions, not only affect his own absolute position, but exercise a powerful influence upon the character and destiny of those by whom he may be surrounded or succeeded upon the busy stage of life.

The history of her patriotic and eminent sons is an important part of a nation's inheritance. Each generation owes to those that follow it the record of the great names and the illustrious deeds which adorn its era, and which may instruct in the great duties of life, and stimulate to their zealous and honorable performance. And of this record the biography of distinguished soldiers, civilians, and scholars is at once the most interesting and effective. It is not the grand outlines of history that make upon the mind the most definite and lively impression. It is its minuter details. We sympathize less with masses than with individuals. A striking incident in the life of a single hero may excite intense interest, and do more to illustrate the elements of character and the principles of patriotism than would the *outline* history of a whole campaign or of an entire age. The general historian frames the skeleton; the biographer furnishes the flesh and blood and vitality.

But it is not only with reference to the virtues and wisdom of men that biography is important. Even the records of human vices and follies have also their salutary uses. They serve to guard us against those evils into which others may have fallen, and to secure to us those temporal and eternal blessings which are too often wantonly disregarded, and perhaps irretrievably lost.

The value of biography, as a study for the young, has always been highly appreciated; but it has been too much the fashion to direct our youth to the lives of Plutarch rather than to the achievements of men in our own times. Not only is much of the moral force, which it is the peculiar advantage of biography to impart, lost by the purely ideal aspect in which the youthful imagination contemplates a Grecian sage or a Roman hero, but the spheres of distinction in which they were illustrious were so different from those to which men are now attracted, that very little either of wholesome incentive or needed encouragement can be derived from them. Great antiquity, far-off distance of time, invests the character of even a common mind with a glory beautiful as a picture, but noways encouraging as an example. We look at them to admire, but not to imitate. In full harmony, therefore, not only with the spirit of the age, but no less with the wants of our nature, we are gratified to see a growing tendency toward the publication and study of a cotemporaneous biography, not in a few departments of life only, but in every walk in which the human mind may usefully and honorably exert itself. Every pursuit needs the encouragement of successful examples.

Of the two classes of biography—one, of men of such eminence in the political, literary, or religious world as to awaken the admiration without inspiring the hopeful emulation of the reader; the other, of characters in humbler walks, whose success in life may serve to instruct and stimulate the zeal of the most obscure—those of the latter sort, though less brilliant, are often more useful. The life of Norman Smith, the Hartford saddler, will carry lessons of practical wisdom and of sound Christian morality into the business and bosoms of tens of thousands of the sons of toil, while the more eventful career of a more public man may have fewer available lessons for the masses of youthful aspirants in the ordinary spheres of life. Let the models for the study of young Americans be such as they may safely and hopefully imitate, and their power will be none the less that they are not beyond their reach. The great lesson to be instilled into the youthful mind is that of industry and fidelity in whatever position in life. The faithful discharge of present duty in an humble sphere is the surest road to promotion. Here lies the clue to wealth, fame—all that is worth seeking in this life, and perhaps all that is valuable in immortal hopes.

The department of biography is crowded with the lives of men distinguished in war, politics, science, literature, and the professions. All the embellishments of rhetoric and the imagination have been essayed to captivate, stimulate, and direct into these "upper walks of life," as they are entitled, the youthful mind and ambition of the country. Not content to make the academies and higher educational institutions hotbeds and nurseries to germinate and train aspirations for fame, military and civic, the most brilliant achievements in the field, the forum, the hall, and at the bar, of the great men of the past and present, have been exhibited in colors warm and glowing, to charm and inspire. Example has been added to precept; the teachings of the lecture-room have been enforced by illustrations from real life, and the chaplet of glory and renown has been held up as the great and only prize.

The result of this system is manifest, and by no means fortunate. The ranks of the professions are filled and overflowing. Pettifoggers, quacks, pedants, demagogues, and militia officers are manufactured by wholesale. Thousands of young men of respectable abilities, entirely capable of achieving competence and character in the useful and more unpretending employments, are annually allured into professions for which they are entirely unsuited, and in which they can never succeed. Disappointment and idleness, or charlatanry and vice, are unfortunately the too frequent results, instead of thrift, independence, and respectability flowing from wiser counsels.

To instill into the minds and hearts of the young respect for great attainments, reverence for great virtues, and to excite the generous emulation by holding up, as examples for admiration and imitation, the lives of the wise, and great, and good, is commendable and right. But the field of example should be extended, and lessons on industry, energy, usefulness, virtue, honor, the true aims of life and the true sources of happiness, should be gathered and enforced from all the various provinces of human labor, however humble. Our country is eminently in need of increased intelligence in commerce, agriculture, and mechanism.

Those great divisions of labor should be rendered not only lucrative and respectable, as they are, but honorable and attractive to the young in all classes of society. The lives of eminent merchants, farmers, manufacturers, mechanics—of all who by honest labor have achieved distinguished success in the different occupations—should be written, and commended to the young men of the republic. The path of labor and usefulness should be indicated as the highway to honor.

The individual who devotes his time and talents to such pursuits as render him useful to his country, while, at the same time, they accomplish for him, personally, the objects of honorable employment, is "performing well his part in the drama of life." To succeed, in such designs, is to deserve the gratitude and admiration of the world.

Instruction is often most effectually given by example. Not a few men, it is believed, pass their lives in obscurity and want, mainly because, from the unfavorable circumstances in which their lives commence, they pass the period of youth under a vague but general impression that eminence, in any important respect, is unattainable by them; and hence they form no fixed *purpose* to attain it. A better means of dissipating this delusion, and of rousing the minds of young men and lads, in the humbler walks of life, to high and noble aims, and of stimulating them to the achievement of such aims, can hardly be adopted than holding before them the example and history of others who have pushed their way upward into affluence, honor, and usefulness, from amid circumstances not less discouraging than their own.

This work exhibits, as all biography will, that those who are most successful in obtaining honors, public respect, and wealth, have not pursued these as the ends of their labors, but have obtained them as incidents to active virtues. When we make reputation, honor, or riches the *motives* instead of the *rewards* of our conduct, we reverse the order which Providence has established, and fail of obtaining what we are perversely seeking. When Solomon was asked what he most desired, he said, " Give thy servant an understanding heart to judge thy people. And God said unto him, Because thou hast asked this thing, and hast not asked for thyself long life, nor riches, nor the life of thine enemies, lo! I have given thee a wise and an understanding heart; so that there was none like thee before, neither after thee shall any arise like unto thee. And I have also given thee what thou hast not asked, both riches and honor." He asked to perform well his duties, and the performance brought with it riches and honor as incidents of duty.

If a lawyer discharges well and faithfully his legal duties, riches and honor will follow as natural incidents; but should he make riches the object of his efforts, he will not necessarily perform faithfully his legal duties, but by subordinating them to avarice, he will lose his business and character without in the end obtaining the riches thus viciously pursued.

A politician who interests himself usefully in public matters will obtain official station as an incident of his usefulness; but should he make office the motive of his political conduct, he will be as often uselessly busy as actively useful, and give offense by officiousness rather than gain favor by usefulness. So, an officer who discharges faithfully his public duties will obtain popularity as an incident of his faithfulness; but should he pursue popularity as the object of his actions, he will not necessarily discharge faithfully his duties, but will subordinate them to his popularity, and so waver in his conduct and fluctuate in his sentiments as to fail in reaching the desired end. A physician who skillfully performs his practice will obtain celebrity and patronage as incidents of his skill; but should he pursue celebrity and patronage as motives, he will magnify slight ailments, that he may obtain the merit of achieving astonishing recoveries. He will publish miraculous cures which never occurred, and he will be contemned rather than obtain patronage and celebrity.

A like principle pervades, necessarily, all the business occupations of life. The organization of man, of society, and of the universe are alike favorable to honesty and virtuous conduct. Duties faithfully discharged lead to wealth and honor; duties selfishly performed to poverty and disgrace. There is not a name in this work whose life is not illustrative of these truths.

Under a government like ours, where there are no privileged classes, and where no hereditary distinctions exist, it very frequently happens that the most important and responsible offices are held by those of whom it may very properly be said, they have been the pioneers of their own fortunes—men who have received little or no assistance from wealthy or influential relatives, but who are indebted for their success in life to their own industry and perseverance. Indeed, this is generally the case in the United States, and it is easy to see why it should be so. Native talent is not confined to any class of society; though, as a general rule, it may reasonably be presumed that the children of intellectual parents will have more natural talent than the children of the ignorant, the stupid, or the imbecile. The sons of the wealthy, however, or of those who occupy situations of great power or influence, are too often found to rely upon the wealth or the influence of their parents, and seldom acquire those habits of industry, perseverance, and energy which are essential to success. On the other hand, those whose parents are poor, or belong to the middle classes of society, being early taught the necessity of relying upon their own exertions, will be more apt to acquire that information and those business habits which alone can fit them for the discharge of important public trusts, and that industry and perseverance which usually insure success.

Success, though sometimes apparently flowing from the caprices of fortune, is, after all, the surest test of real merit; and it is encouraging to every young man who, repining not at the accidents of his birth, looks up with a trustful spirit to higher spheres of usefulness and fame, to know that others have gone before him with prospects no fairer than his own, and have triumphed, The success of others gives us confidence in ourselves. What they have done, we may do; and thus the example of those who have successfully trod any of the diversified paths of life becomes the mental heritage of every aspiring spirit, more valuable than houses or lands. It is the capital which plumes the pinions of hope—the stock in trade which gives confidence to the mind, when failure might else point to despair.

To write a memoir of a living man—that is, to present a faithful record of his life and acts; of the impressions he has made, and is still making, upon his times; of the bias he has given, and is still giving, to public sentiment; and to indicate the logical deductions which may reasonably be drawn, prospectively, from the influence he has exercised, and is still exercising, upon men and things around him—is a task of no ordinary difficulty and delicacy. That the opposite opinions and discordant statements of his acts, as determined by the interests, passions, and prejudices of individuals, will be investigated with the sternness and impartiality that the composition of history, in its most extensive view, demands, is not to be expected; nor, from the very nature of the task, can full force and measurement be given to the inferences which his actions will assuredly develop. It remains, then, for his cotemporary biographer only to present an accurate narrative of events, in their natural and unbroken sequence; neither suppressing nor concealing important circumstances, nor giving undue prominence to trivial incidents; limiting his philosophy to effects already produced, and to probable future conclusions; carefully avoiding, however, in deducing them, the semblance even of crude or vague speculation. But, in this limited field of narration, he must none the less, if he really designs to enlighten and instruct mankind, studiously aim at "that nicety and strength of reflection, and that subtlety and discernment in the unraveling of character, and that choice of circumstances necessary for enlivening the whole narration," which Addison tells us is essential for placing a public character in a proper light, that the merit designed to be perpetuated may not be handed down to posterity with disadvantage.

As artists set a peculiar value on Allston's great *unfinished* painting of Belshazzar's feast, because the different parts of it show his method of working out a picture, from the first rough chalk outline to the last finishing touch of the pencil, so a biography is most valuable which traces every step in the unfolding and development of character. The results of industrious life lie open and obvious around us, but the means of attaining these results, and the habits of mind by which character is formed, are more secret.

There are few whose lives are not worthy of record, and in whose history something may not be found useful as a rule or example for others. Besides, it is a duty we owe to ourselves and our posterity to cherish and keep alive the remembrance of those who have, by their own energy and industry, without the aid of wealth or hereditary influence, attained a position which makes them ornaments of society and guide-posts to honor and fame.

A FEW NOTICES OF THE PRESS.

The *New York National Democrat* says:

So far as we know, this is the first book of any sort that purposes to hand down to after times, in an authentic form, the portraits and characters of men distinguished in the walks of private as well as of public life.

The author's conception of the great work of living biographies was fortunate in the extreme. No other plan of the kind has before been so fully undertaken and so well carried out. We can not but regard this large and splendid production as one of the most remarkable and valuable this country has yet seen.

The *New York Tribune* says:

It exhibits a remarkable catalogue of self-made men, and illustrates the steps by which they arose from obscurity to wealth and consideration. It is pleasing to remark that the individuals of whom sketches are here given are indebted for their success in life to genuine, sturdy, straightforward qualities; to energy, diligence, and enterprise, rather than to the arts by which so many manage to swindle themselves into a good reputation.

In a recent notice the *New York Commercial Advertiser* says:

The portraits are all engraved from daguerreotypes, in the finest style of the art, and are undoubtedly correct. We can vouch for the remarkable fidelity of the likenesses of those persons with whose faces we are familiar. This truly national work is creditable to the ability and enterprise of Mr. Livingston, and should adorn every public and private library in the country. His plan is to "no creed or class confined," but embraces clergymen, lawyers, doctors, soldiers, statesmen, financiers, merchants, manufacturers, and farmers—in short, distinguished living representatives of every department of American society. To expatiate on the value of such a work would be superfluous, as it must commend itself to universal favor.

The *Boston Daily Bee* says:

The volumes contain exquisitely finished steel plate engravings, which alone are worth far more than the cost of the work. It would be a tame compliment to remark that these portraits and memoirs form one of the most interesting works of the age. They are more—they are the most valuable. Here is a vast amount of information, which must have cost immense toil, and which none but an intellectual giant could or would have collected. One remarkable and most encouraging fact shines from every page of these volumes, viz.: that nearly all our men of eminence have risen from the ranks of the masses; risen by the most indomitable energy, industry, and integrity.

We cordially recommend Mr. Livingston's great American work. It should be on every table and in every library, that the young of our land may draw inspiration and courage from the noble men it portrays.

The *Washington Daily Union* says:

By a large expenditure of means he has attained to that point which he had in view when he commenced his labors upon it—that is, to make it a work which, while it might elicit admiration and praise as to its mechanical arrangement, should at the same time be a true historical record of the lives and services of those eminent citizens whose portraits adorn its columns.

JUST PUBLISHED,

PORTRAITS OF EMINENT AMERICANS NOW LIVING; including PRESIDENT PIERCE AND HIS CABINET: with Biographical and Historical Memoirs of their Lives and Actions. By John Livingston, of the New York Bar. Complete in one volume.

This volume contains 550 pages, octavo, with 50 fine steel portraits made from daguerreotypes, expressly for the work. The engravings alone have cost over five thousand dollars.

☞ Price $5, well bound in cloth, full gilt. It may be had of all booksellers in the city of New York, or will be sent by mail, free of postage, to any part of the United States, by Mr. Livingston, on receipt of five dollars.

CONTENTS.

STATES ALPHABETICALLY ARRANGED.

Engd. by H.B. Hall.

Franklin Pierce

PRESIDENT OF THE UNITED STATES.

Engd. for Biographical Sketches of Eminent Americans.

BIOGRAPHICAL AND HISTORICAL MEMOIRS.

FRANKLIN PIERCE,

PRESIDENT OF THE UNITED STATES.

His father—Benjamin Pierce—was born in the year 1757, at the village of Chelmsford—now the flourishing manufacturing city of Lowell—in Massachusetts. Having had the misfortune to lose both his parents in early life, he became the ward of an uncle, under whom he was brought up to the frugal lot of a New England farmer's boy in those early days.

When but eighteen years old, whilst at the plough, the news reached him of the massacres of Lexington and Concord, and leaving the share in the unfinished furrow, he hastily seized his uncle's gun and equipments, resolving to avenge the blood of these martyrs, or add his own to his country's cause.

He enlisted in the continental army, and was present as a private in its ranks at the bloody action of Bunker's Hill.

He served throughout the whole of the Revolutionary War, and returned at the end of seven years, the commander of a company. He was retained in the army until its final disbandment at West Point in 1784, and then retired; his only reward, the consciousness of having well performed the patriot's duty; his rank, and his pay in the continental currency, then almost worthless.

In the spring of 1786, he built himself a log cabin, and commenced the clearing and cultivation of a tract of wild land, which he had purchased in the preceding year, whilst employed as agent to explore the district, in the midst of which now stands the town of Hillsborough. In the succeeding year, he took to his new home, as a wife, Elizabeth Andrews, in whose companionship his enjoyment was brief, for she died within that year, leaving to his charge a daughter—the present widow of General John McNeil. In 1789, he married Anna Kendrick, who was his loving helpmate in his prime and through his declining years, and who bore him eight children, of whom his present illustrious son was the sixth.

We must beg the patience of the reader to allow us the pleasing task of dwelling for a few moments longer upon the incidents of the life of this revolutionary hero; and not the less for the reason that his position as parent to the personage of whom we shall directly speak, is strikingly illustrative of the fact of hereditary greatness.

Whilst engaged in clearing his wild lands, and performing the first acts of civilization in a portion of his state then so little known, that he had been commissioned to *explore* it in 1786, he received the appointment of Brigade-major of the militia of Hillsborough county, then first organized. In 1789, he was elected to the State Legislature, in which body he held his seat for thirteen successive years, until chosen a Member of the Council; during this period, however, he did not neglect his military duties, but became a Field Officer, and finally General of the militia of the county. In 1801—to show the estimation in which his military talents were held during the administration of the elder Adams—he was offered a high command in the northern division of the army which was proposed to be levied in anticipation of a war with France; but ever faithful to his principles, and inflexibly democratic in his political faith, he refused to be implicated in a policy which he could not approve, and his answer to the gentlemen who pressed his acceptance of the commission, should be emblazoned in letters of gold, and placed conspicuously before his countrymen. "No," replied the patriot, "poor as I am, and acceptable as would be the position under other circumstances, I would sooner go to yonder mountain, dig me a cave, and live on roast potatoes, than be instrumental in promoting the objects for which that army is to be raised!" And it is a singular fact that the same simile should have served another patriot—the partisan Marion—to illustrate his devotion to his principles, when overtures were made to him by British officers.

Another touching incident is related of him. On the 26th of December, 1825—it being his sixty-seventh birth-day—he had prepared a festival for his comrades in arms—the survivors of the Revolution—eighteen of whom, all inhabitants of Hillsborough, assembled at his house. They spent the day in festivity, reviewing the great deeds they had witnessed and helped to do, and in reviving the old sentiments of the era of seventy-six. At nightfall, after a manly and pathetic farewell from their host, they separated, "prepared"—as the old General expressed it—"at the first tap of the shrouded drum, to move and join their beloved Washington, and the rest of their comrades who had fought and bled at their sides."

In 1827, General Benjamin Pierce was elected Governor of the state of New Hampshire. In 1839, he died at the mansion he had built after the original log cabin had become too small for his rising family and fortunes. After having been spared to behold the distinction of his son, he departed this life at the ripe age of eighty-one, in perfect peace, and, until within a few hours of his death, in the full possession of his intellectual powers.

'How sleep the dead, who sink to rest
With all their country's honors blest?"

Franklin Pierce was born at Hillsborough, New Hampshire, on the 23d day of November, 1804, and, upon his election to the Presidency, had just reached his forty-eighth year.

At the time of his birth, and for years after, his father was the most active and public-spirited man within his sphere, and, from what we have set down as the character of General Benjamin Pierce, it may well be said, "If any man is bound, by birth and youthful training, to show himself a brave, faithful, and able citizen of his native country, it is the son of such a father."

At the commencement of the war of 1812, Franklin Pierce was about eight years of age; his two brothers were in the army, and his half-sister soon after became the wife of Major McNeil. As his father, both in his public capacity as a Member of the Council, and by his great local influence in his own county, lent a strenuous support to the national administration, and not only took a prominent part in all public meetings, but was ever ready for the informal discussion of political affairs at places of casual resort, it is not strange that his son, in hearing these discussions, and listening to the argument of his venerated sire, should have become deeply imbued with the principles and sentiment of democratic institutions.

His father having felt the disadvantages of a defective education, determined to afford his son all the opportunities himself had lacked, and sent him early to the Academy of Hancock, and afterwards placed him in that of Francestown, where he resided in the family of Peter Woodbury, the father of the late eminent judge.

He entered Bowdoin College at Brunswick, Maine, in 1820; and amongst his fellow students and associates were men who have since made their mark high in the niche of fame; it will be sufficient to name Professor Stowe, Nathaniel Hawthorne, the pious Caldwell, and the chivalrous and lamented Cilley. At this College, with such men as these for competitors, he took a highly creditable degree. He was here the Chairman of the Athenian Society, and first displayed his inclination for the

"Pomp and circumstance of glorious war,"

as an officer of a military company composed of his fellow collegians.

Nor is it to his discredit to state, that, like Webster, and nearly all the distinguished men of the region from which he sprang, he taught a country school during one of his winter vacations: kings have learned to rule from as humble a sphere, for

"Men are but children of an older growth."

After leaving college, Franklin Pierce became a student of law in the office of Judge Woodbury of Portsmouth, from thence he went to the Law School at Northampton in Massachusetts, and finished his preparatory studies in the office of Judge Parker at Amherst. In the year 1827 he was admitted to the bar, and began to practise in his native town. He was not very successful in his earliest cases, but a proof of his indomitable will and self-reliance is recorded in the remark made by him to a friend who wished to console him on the loss of a case: "I will try nine hundred and ninety-nine cases, and if I fail, just as I have to-day, I will try the thousandth." He felt the strength within him—he knew that time would bring it out.

In 1829 he was elected a Representative of his native town to the Legislature of the State. He served in that body four years, the last two years as speaker, to which office he was chosen by a vote greater than two thirds.

He was sent to the Congress of the United States in 1833, and his Congressional life, though it made but little show, was full of labor directed to substantial objects. He was a member of the Judiciary and other important Committees; and the drudgery of the Committee room, where so much of the real public business of the country is performed, fell in large measure to his lot. General Jackson, the man of his choice, and to whom his first political faith had been given, when a youthful combatant he had entered the political arena, then occupied the Presidential Chair, and to the sustaining of his measures were all his powers exerted; and, in after years, when the Old Hero was about passing away, he remarked, as if a glimpse of the future had been granted to him, and his enlarged vision then comprehended what has since come to pass, "The interests of the country will be safe in the hands of Franklin Pierce."

He continued in the House of Representatives four years, and in 1837 was elected to the Senate; and after performing services there, for which his country has proved herself grateful, in June, 1842, he resigned his seat and retired to the sweets of domestic life, taking up again his profession to repair by its practice the inroads which the public service had made upon his means. In 1834 he had married a daughter of the Rev. Doctor Appleton, a former President of Bowdoin College. Three sons had now been born to him, and to this increase of family, and his well known predilection for a domestic life, may be attributed his sudden and unlooked for resignation of the honorable position of Senator, which upon its announcement filled the Senate Chamber with surprise, and in its fulfilment left a void in that body long sensibly felt.

In 1838 he removed from Hillsborough to Concord, where he sedulously applied himself to the duties of his profession, and where he fulfilled the promise of his youth. Nor had he now occasion to "try again;"—he had found the strength, he *then knew* he possessed—time and application had brought it out—and his reputation as a lawyer is surpassed by none in a state where such a standing is not easily obtained.

In 1846 he was offered by President Polk the post of Attorney-General of the United States, which he modestly declined in consideration of the interests of his clients, and the health of Mrs. Pierce, thus showing his devotion to those who had intrusted their affairs to his keeping; and that most beautiful trait of his character, which is in accordance with the whole tenor of his life.

He had previously been tendered by the Governor the appointment of U. S. Senator, which he had declined for similar reasons; and as if fortune would still persist in thrusting honors upon him, he was nominated by a democratic convention for Governor, and again refused the distinction.

In his letter to President Polk, declining the Attorney-Generalship, this passage occurs: "When I resigned my seat in the Senate in 1842, I did so with the fixed purpose never again to be voluntarily separated from my family for any considerable length of time, except at the call of my country in time of war." And this contingency did soon present itself, for shortly after, in 1847, when the State of New Hampshire was called upon to furnish its proportion of troops for the Mexican War, Mr. Pierce, true to his pledge and democratic principles, enrolled himself a member of one of the first Volunteer Companies of Concord, and performed the duties of a private in the ranks. Merit like his, however, could not long remain concealed, and on the passage of the Bill for the increase of the army, he received the appointment of Colonel of the Ninth Regiment, which was the quota of New England towards the ten regiments to be raised; and in March of the same year was commissioned Brigadier-General in the Army.

On the 27th of May he embarked at Newport with his command, and after a tedious passage of thirty days, arrived at Vera Cruz, where he found that dreadful scourge—the Vomito—raging violently. Anxious for the health of his men, he had them conveyed directly from the transports to Viraga—an extensive sandy beach upon the gulf, about two miles beyond the walls of the city. From hence he found great difficulty in taking up his line of march, a stampede having taken place among the mules collected for his train, in which some fifteen hundred were lost. On the 16th of July, after a delay of nearly three weeks, during which time many of his best officers and men were victims to the Vomito, he started for the main army, with animals so intractable that he was only able to advance a few miles before darkness compelled him to bivouac for the safety of his train. The next morning he commenced his march at four o'clock, and reached Santa Fé at eight, where, finding the heat too oppressive for both men and beasts, he remained in camp until four P.M., when he pushed on, and arrived at San Juan the same evening, in the midst of a drenching rain.

In his march from Telema Nueva to the Puente Nacionale he had an engagement with the Guerillas, in which he speaks highly of the conduct of his men, then for the first time under fire. The enemy's loss was set down by themselves at forty, whilst of his command but six were wounded and seven horses killed. This action was creditable to his skill as a general, not only in regard to the superiority of the force he repulsed—for the whole country, as far back as Jalapa, was swarming with these independent warriors, intimate with every mountain path and secret defile—but also as to the manner in which his troops were placed, as shown in the small loss sustained.

At the National Bridge he again found the enemy prepared to dispute his progress, having thrown a barricade across the bridge, and making a strong demonstration in the village beyond, where their lancers were in position. These, however, were soon dispersed, and he took possession of the village, locating his head-quarters at one of the splendid villas of Santa Anna.

During the action he had a very narrow escape, an escopete ball removing the rim of his sombrero, which he only notices from the inconvenience of "leaving his head exposed to the rays of the sun."

At the Plan del Rio he found the entire main arch of the viaduct blown up, and a span of about sixty feet removed; this difficulty he soon overcame, and in less than four hours a road was constructed over which the men and waggons passed safely.

From Plan del Rio he proceeded to Jalapa, which was reached on the 25th of July, and thence he continued on to La Hoya, where he arrived on the 29th, without molestation. But now the effects of the climate, exposure, and improper indulgence in fruit, which the strictest discipline could not prevent their obtaining, began to tell terribly on his troops, and over four hundred of his command were upon the sick list. On the first of August, he encamped under the walls of the castle of Perote, where he halted several days to repair damages, procure supplies, and give rest to his troops. He left his sick at the castle, receiving from the garrison an equal number of convalescents, and having thus recruited his command, reached the main army at Puebla on the 7th of August, with twenty-four hundred men, in fine order, and without the loss of a single waggon.

Upon the arrival of this reinforcement, General Scott broke up his camp, and began his march upon the Capital.

On the 19th the sanguinary conflict of Contreras took place. In this action, whilst a portion of the American forces were ordered to move against the left flank of the Mexican army, then in strong position under Valencia, to divert his attention from their movements, a vigorous assault was made upon his front, and General Pierce's brigade was included in the attacking party. The assault, at first intended as a partial demonstration, was so desperately resisted, that it soon became a severe engagement,—and, as the Mexican artillery in full force, and strongly entrenched, poured showers of round shot, grape, cannister, and shell, upon the little bands of Americans, who, from the nature of the ground were unable to bring their artillery to bear, their position assumed the character of a "forlorn hope."

General Pierce, in the midst of this fire, leaped his horse upon an eminence, and addressed the troops as they passed—reminding them of the honor of their country, and of the victory their steady valor would contribute to achieve. Pressing forward to the head of the column, his horse slipped among the rocks, thrust his foot into a crevice, and fell, breaking his own leg, and crushing his rider heavily beneath him. When his orderly approached he was stunned and nearly insensible, and being extricated from his dangerous position he was found to be severely bruised, and his left knee badly sprained from the weight of the animal in falling upon it. Whilst his orderly was assisting him to the shelter of a projecting rock, a shell falling close beside them exploded, covering them both with earth; in a calm tone General Pierce remarked, "that was a lucky miss."

Doctor Ritchie, attached to his brigade, was fortunately at hand, and having administered to him as well as circumstances would permit, strongly remonstrated against his rejoining his troops in such a condition; but the general, supported by his orderly, with great pain and difficulty reached the battery of Captain McGruder, where finding the horse of a wounded officer, at his own urgent request, he was assisted to mount. In answer to a remark that he would be unable to keep his seat, he replied "then you must tie me on," and rode forward into the battle.

General Pierce remained in the saddle until eleven o'clock that night, when beneath a torrent of rain, destitute of a tent or other protection, without food or refreshment, he stretched himself upon an ammunition waggon, where he lay, prevented by the pain of his wounded limb from gaining the least repose. At early dawn he was again in the saddle at the head of his brigade, which had taken its former position in front of the enemy. Soon after the Mexican camp was stormed, and in the short space of seventeen minutes had fallen into the hands of its assailants, together with a multitude of prisoners.

The remnant of the routed army fled towards Churubusco, and Pierce led his brigade in pursuit until they reached the strong positions there, and at San Antonio.

As Santa Anna, after this defeat, appeared to be anxious to withdraw his force towards the city, in order to intercept this movement, Pierce's brigade, with other troops, was ordered to pursue a route and attack the enemy in the rear. When he approached the Commander-in-Chief to receive his orders, General Scott remarked—"Pierce, my dear fellow, you are badly injured, you are not fit to be in the saddle." "Yes, general, I am," replied Pierce, "in a case like this." "You cannot touch your foot to the stirrup," said Scott. "One of them I can," answered Pierce. The general looked again at Pierce's almost disabled figure, and seemed on the point of taking his irrevocable resolution. "You are rash, General Pierce," said he, "we shall lose you and we cannot spare you, it is my duty to order you back to San Augustine." "For God's sake! General," exclaimed Pierce—"don't say that, this is our last great battle, and I must lead my brigade."

The Commander-in-Chief made no remonstrance, but gave the order for Pierce to advance.

The way lay through thick standing corn, and over marshy ground, intersected with ditches, which were filled or partially so, with water; over some of the narrower of these Pierce leaped his horse. When the brigade had advanced about a mile, however, it found its progress impeded by a ditch ten or twelve feet wide, and six or eight feet deep. It being impossible to leap it, General Pierce was lifted from his saddle, and in some incomprehensible manner, hurt as he was, contrived to wade or scramble across this obstacle, leaving his horse on the hither side. The troops were now under fire. In the excitement of the battle, he forgot his injuries and hurried forward, leading the brigade a distance of two or three hundred yards. But the exhaustion of his frame, and particularly the anguish of his knee, made more intolerable by such free use of it, was greater than any strength of nerve, or any degree of mental energy, could struggle against. He fell, faint and almost insensible, within full range of the enemy's fire. It was proposed to bear him off the field, but as some of his soldiers approached to lift him he became aware of their purpose, and was partially revived by his determination to resist it. "No," said he, with all the strength he had left, "don't carry me off! leave me here;" and there he lay under the tremendous fire of Churubusco, until the enemy in total rout was driven from the field.

Immediately after this victory, Santa Anna sent a flag of truce proposing an armistice with a view to negotiations for peace, and General Pierce was appointed by the Commander-in-Chief one of the commissioners on our part, together with Generals Quitman and Persifer F. Smith, to arrange the terms of this armistice. Pierce was unable to walk or to mount his horse without assistance, when intelligence of his appointment reached him. He had not removed his spurs, nor slept an hour for two nights, but he immediately obeyed the summons, was assisted into the saddle and rode to Tacubaya, where, at the house of the British Consul General, the American and Mexican Commissioners were assembled; the conference began late in the afternoon, and continued until four o'clock the next morning, when the articles were signed. Pierce then proceeded to the quarters of General Worth, where he obtained a short repose.

The armistice was of short duration, Santa Anna having resorted to his favorite *ruse* to prevent the American troops from taking possession of the capital, which might have been entered immediately after the battle of Churubusco.

The next battle was that of Molino del Rey, one of the most obstinately contested and sanguinary conflicts of the whole campaign. In this action General Worth with three thousand troops attacked and routed fourteen thousand Mexicans, driving them under the protection of the guns of Chapultepec. General Pierce was ordered with his brigade to the support of Worth. With his usual alacrity he pushed forward, but arrived just in time to see the gallant Worth master of the field; but doubtless the ardor and rapidity of his approach greatly added to the panic of the Mexicans, and although he did not assist in their defeat, yet he had the satisfaction of interposing his forces between Worth and the retreating enemy, and thus drew upon himself the fire of Chapultepec. A shell from the castle bursting near his horse so startled the animal that he came near plunging over an adjacent precipice. Still under fire, his brigade was actively engaged in removing the wounded, and securing the captured ammunition, and whilst thus occupied he led a portion of his command to repel the attacks of the enemy's skirmishers.

Although still suffering from his injuries and over-exertion, General Pierce had continued to act with his brigade, and on the day previous to the battle of Chapultepec had occupied the field of Molino del Rey. Contrary to expectation it was found that the enemy had withdrawn his forces, and Pierce having remained upon the field until noon, when it became certain that the contemplated attack would not take place until the following day, returned to the quarters of General Worth; here his strength, exerted beyond the powers of human endurance, gave way, and he remained unable to move from his bed for thirty-six hours. In that time the glorious battle of Chapultepec had been gained, in which his brigade behaved most gallantly and suffered severely, and Colonel Ransom, in leading the ninth regiment, was shot. An obstinate defence was now made at the gates of Belen and San Cosmo, and it was expected that it would be necessary to storm the city. When this was told to General Pierce, he made an attempt to rise from his bed and dress himself, but was prevailed upon by Captain Hardcastle to remain and husband his strength until there should be immediate occasion for its use. In this he appeared to acquiesce, but arose in the night, and making his way to the trenches reported himself to General Quitman, with whom a part of his brigade was acting. Quitman's share in the anticipated assault, it was supposed, owing to the position which his troops occupied, would be more perilous than that of Worth. But the war was ended. The campaign had closed with Chapultepec. The Mexicans had abandoned their capital. The victorious Americans took possession, and soon the stars and stripes were floating proudly over the "Halls of the Montezumas."

General Pierce remained in Mexico until December, when the war being concluded, and negotiations for peace nearly settled, he returned to his loved home, and resigning his commission applied himself again to the practice of law.

In 1850, in pursuance of a vote of the people of New Hampshire, a convention was assembled at Concord for a revision of the constitution, and General Pierce was elected its president by an almost unanimous ballot. In this convention he was active in his exertions to procure the repeal of the illiberal Catholic test,—so long a stain on the statute-book of that State—and aided by Judge Woodbury and other democratic members, attained his purpose as far as the Convention possessed any power or responsibility in the matter.

On the 12th of June, 1852, the democratic convention at Baltimore nominated Franklin Pierce as their candidate for the presidency of the United States, and in the fall of the same year he received the vote of nearly all the electoral colleges—an unanimity unparalleled since the days of Washington; and on the fourth day of March last he was publicly inaugurated the president of the United States.

The professional qualifications of General Pierce as a practising lawyer were of the highest character. A spectator who witnesses an interesting trial in a court of justice, while gratified by the intellectual exhibition there presented, can hardly realize the training by which the gladiators in the legal arena have acquired their strength and skill. Legal knowledge, ready to be used at a moment's warning, self-possession, experience of human nature—all the energies of a well stored and self-poised mind, are called into constant requisition in every important trial. These qualifications Mr. Pierce in an eminent degree combined. He had, besides, the advantage of entering upon his profession with a finished academical and legal education. By severe study he had mastered the science of law, till his mind played with its subtlest distinctions—but he never neglected close and untiring preparation for each particular cause. Those who knew his mode of transacting business, remarked the careful manner in which his jury-trials were prepared. Many of these were, of course, long, intricate, and involved with many embarrassments. Such cases demand the most minute preparation, and it has often been observed that General Pierce was remarkable for anticipating difficulties, and making provisions for contingencies likely to arise in the course of a trial, which were unforeseen by others. None but the practising lawyer can fully understand the value of this peculiar talent. Every important trial is full of surprises, where the light-minded, superficial, and timid advocate is often overcome, and a good cause irrevocably lost by one fatal mis-step.

In his addresses to the jury, as an advocate, Mr. Pierce had few equals and no superiors among his cotemporaries. His language was fluent, copious, and select—his manner and attitude peculiarly graceful and dignified—his voice flexible, sonorous, and entirely under his control. With logical clearness he presented his strong points to the minds of the jury, and urged them upon their consideration with that persuasive eloquence which it is difficult to resist.

The defence of innocence—the assertion of right—the exposure and punishment of fraud—and the redress of wrong—these were the occasions which roused to the utmost the energies of his mind, and furnished full scope for the exhibition of his uncommon power as an advocate. At such times, when the full exertion of his strength was demanded, his eloquence rose with the occasion in power and energy, and bore along with its irresistible torrent the convictions of his hearers.

In addressing a jury, his aim seemed to be, first of all, to gain their entire and willing confidence, by evincing his sincerity throughout the whole course of the trial. He would convince them that he was honest as a man; and that he was honest as a lawyer in advocating the interests of his client. Thus he the more easily carried the jury along with him to the desired conclusion. They were made to feel that he was really endeavoring to aid and facilitate their efforts to find the true state of the case; and were thus disarmed of the suspicion too often well founded, that the advocate is practising the subtilty of his art only to conceal and distort the truth. In this course, Mr. Pierce is worthy of all praise, and of all imitation.

In the form and texture of his address, he was brief, comprehensive, and strong: seizing upon the main points of his case and wasting no strength on the unimportant or inconsiderable ones. By precept as well as by example he disapproved of the interminable and undigested arguments now so common at the bar; obstructing, as they do, the general administration of justice, and wearying out the patience of judges and jurors; and finally, not unfrequently ruining the cause itself which is thus advocated.

Fully recognising the principle that his profession could only be used for moral purposes, Mr. Pierce was always anxious to prevent litigation where the ends of justice could be gained without this resort. With this view he was in the habit of advising his clients to settle their disputes by conciliation and by mutual agreement. And he was often successful in bringing about the results which he desired. In many cases, however, the cause of his client would be so palpably just as to leave no room for delay in embracing its advocacy; in others, there was such a complication of facts and circumstances, as well as of precedents, that the trial alone could determine which party was in the right; and yet in other cases, more doubtful, the client was still entitled to an impartial application of the law to the facts which might be established by an open hearing of both sides. It was, however, his constant wish and effort to bring about the settlement of cases, where this was possible, without their proceeding to the expense and other evils of a public trial.

Did our space permit, we could with pleasure say more of Mr. Pierce's qualities, mental and moral. In manners he is characterized by dignified simplicity; in conversation, by earnestness and truthfulness; and in all his intercourse and business with men, by integrity. In his reverence for sincerity and truth, he has ever despised those arts by which ambitious men court the populace, or conciliate the individual. In all the walks of life, public as well as private, he has been content to appear what he is, and to be estimated simply for his worth. And if honors have flowed in upon him, they have been the unbought homage which the human heart still pays to virtue and talent exerted in the public service. Imbued from childhood with a deep reverence for goodness and truth in others, it is but natural that these qualities should be conspicuous in himself. And his character might be summed up in these two words, integrity and earnestness—integrity, or a perfect harmony between the outward and inward life, pervaded and quickened by moral earnestness. With a character thus informed and moulded, it is not to be wondered, that, in the course of his professional and public life, no act can be pointed at which sullies the honored name he bears.

This sketch would be incomplete, and lack its highest significance, if it did not tell those who may read it, that Mr. Pierce is eminently a religious man. He was carefully educated in the religious principles which distinguished the first settlers of New England, and in early manhood, he made a public profession of his faith in Christ. Through all his subsequent life, he has stood before angels and men a witness to the truth and the joys of religion. His convictions of the truth of Christianity, and of its adaptation to the moral necessities of man, have grown with his growth, and strengthened with his strength. For many years, it has been his daily habit to read and ponder the Oracles of Truth.

As we have thus briefly recounted the leading facts in the life of General Pierce, before closing this sketch, we may be permitted to indulge in a few remarks upon his character, reviewed from a point which, though overlooked by other biographers, seems to present him more favorably as a *man* and a *Christian*, than all the acts of his public career.

The manner in which he has sustained the three relations of son, husband, and father, proves to the world that General Pierce is not only a great, but a *good* man.

When, in 1842, we see him resigning his seat in the Senate chamber, to enable him to resume the practice of a laborious profession in order to provide for those who were more dear to him than all the world besides; when, again, in declining the highest legal position in the country, we hear him say that a public career was never suited to his taste, that he longed for the quiet of domestic life, and had formed a fixed purpose never again to be voluntarily separated from his family for any length of time, we know he felt that true happiness could not be found except in his own dear domestic circle, and around his own fireside. But, how transient are earthly joys! In 1842, *he had a family: then* two sweet little boys, roseate with the glow of that heavenly innocence to be found only in the child, were sleeping by their mother's side. As he thought of these, the sweetest dreams arose, the tenderest chords of feeling were awakened, tears of joy filled his eyes, and he felt happiness could find no fitter shrine, than in such a home. These were the only unsullied joys of this world; the bliss of home never cloyed—the smiles of his children were always true. But while, day and night, he labored to execute his design, in providing for his little household, the bitterness of fortune suddenly overwhelmed him. He lost a promising child, a beautiful little boy; and this was the second wound that had struck deep to afflict him. This loss having been preceded by that of a son in early infancy, he was now left with only one remaining child. The blow fell so heavily upon himself and his devoted wife, that neither scarcely wished to survive it. But, as Christians, from a due sense of the majesty and goodness of God, they were all submission and resignation to his divine will, neither murmuring at his dispensations, nor for a moment doubting the wisdom of Providence in the regulation of human affairs—though they felt that nothing afterwards could make them happy. Even *now* they cannot conceal from themselves the reason they had to cherish so lovely a child. The graces of his countenance, the sweetness of his expressions, the sparklings of his infant wit, the indications he already gave of a placid temper, caused him to be beloved, even by those who were not his relatives, while it rendered still more severe the greatest affliction a parent can suffer.

After these calamities, there remained to Mr. Pierce his son Benjamin, who was all his pleasure, all his hopes. And indeed, he could be a source of comfort; for, already entered upon his seventh year, it was not blossoms he showed, as his younger brother, but well formed fruits, whose harvest could not fail. A few years passed quickly away, and Benjamin was a youth of twelve. He not only had great inclination to study, but was one of those affectionate boys who win the love and esteem of all. If ever child promised to fulfil the expectations of his friends it was he, whose charming voice and sweet countenance are yet so well remembered. But, as if jealous of our happiness, there seems to reign a secret envy which pleases itself in nipping the bud of our hopes.

In the midst of the congratulations of his countrymen, the last fatal blow came. On a winter's morning the President, his wife, and son, were seated with a feeling of perfect security, for a short journey on a New England railroad. There was a sound like a peal of thunder. The car was dashed against the rocks. General Pierce was childless. The eyes of his dear, his only son, had shut for ever to the light, and the soul had departed. He wept. That son who was to succeed him in all his honors, and share them with him in his lifetime, he was never to see more. The fruits and honors of his laborious life were to be left to strangers.

And now, in the midst of all his triumphs, the secret sting of sadness remains buried in his heart. Providence has so dispensed the good and the evil of life, that every man, whatever his station, or however happy his lot, finds crosses and afflictions which always counterbalance his pleasures. There is no perfect happiness on earth. Prosperity is a dream; glory a mistake; the world a deception, which feeds only vain phantoms, leaving nothing solid in the heart.

God alone can comfort our afflictions; and, in the meditation of his holy law, and submission to his eternal decrees, do the bereaved parents seek those solid consolations which they have never found in the world, and which, while softening their afflictions here below, will secure to them their immortal reward hereafter.

W. L. Marcy

SECRETARY OF STATE.

Engraved for Biographical Sketches of Eminent Americans.

WILLIAM L. MARCY,

SECRETARY OF STATE.

The first settlers of the northern shores of our country were stern men, who, refusing dictation as to their manner of worshipping the Supreme Being, became voluntary exiles from their native land, that in the New World they might offer up their supplications in such a manner as would best conform to their own views of addressing their Creator. And, truly, no grander temple could they have selected—no better cathedral built than the eternal forest surrounding New England's rock-bound coast—where the everlasting anthem ascended from Old Ocean's bosom, and blended with the hymns of praise from those primeval woods.

It is not asserted that the ancestors of the subject of this sketch were numbered amongst the pilgrims of Plymouth rock, or that they there offered up their first thanksgiving; but it is certain that they rank among the first of those who chose New England for their home, and were of that Puritan stock, which, disguise the fact as you may, has given a name and standing to this Confederacy, which only men of such iron will and determination could give. Cast your eye over the illustrious of this Union, and frame a list of those

"Names that were not born to die,"

and note what proportion can be traced back to this old Puritan stock. From Maine to Texas, from Carolina to California, you find its offshoots filling the judicial benches, prominent as merchants, useful as mechanics, and in every way performing the duties of good citizens.

In tracing back the ancestry of our distinguished fellow citizen as far as is necessary for us to go, we find a paternal progenitor, Moses Marcy, born in Woodstock, Connecticut, who married there in the year 1723, and removed in 1732 to New-Medfield, afterwards called Sturbridge, where he became the father of a family of eleven children.

He appears to have been a prominent citizen of that town, having built the first grist mill, which, although it may be sneered at now, was then no mean attempt; for in referring to Clark's historical sketch of Sturbridge we find that the principal diet of the inhabitants was at that time *boiled beans*, "which they usually prepared on the evening of one day in sufficient quantities for the breakfast and dinner of the next." He was Colonel of Militia, and the first representative sent from the town to the General Court, and, as Clark relates of him, during the old French War, he repeatedly fitted out soldiers for the army upon his own responsibility, and from his own private resources.

When the revolutionary war took place, he was too far advanced in life to take part in the active scenes of that struggle, but his counsel and advice were never withheld, and his sons and grandsons represented him well and bravely, on the battle-fields of liberty.

He died October 9, 1779, at the age of seventy-two, leaving an honorable name, a large estate, and a numerous posterity.

A grandson of this Colonel Moses Marcy was the father of the subject of our notice. He married Ruth Learned, a descendant of the earliest settlers of Sturbridge; and in that portion of the town, now known as Southbridge, on the 12th day of December, 1786, William L. Marcy was born. He received the rudiments cf knowledge in the schools of his native town, and at the proper age was sent to the Academy at Leicester. It was at this time that party spirit ran high throughout the Union, but especially in the New England States, where the opposition to the republican principles of Thomas Jefferson was bitter in the extreme; and the politics of his preceptor being strongly federalist, the school naturally took its tone from its principal; whilst young Marcy, being of a republican family, and prominent in the advocacy of those principles, was made to suffer for his opinions by exclusion from a society formed for literary and social purposes, the members of which defended Federalist doctrines. From this academy he entered Brown University at Providence, R.I., where he graduated with high honor in 1808.

When about twenty-two years of age he removed to Troy in the State of New York, where, after concluding his studies, he commenced the practice of the law; and it was here too, that he made his *debut* on the political stage.

At the commencement of the war of 1812, being an officer of a military company belonging to the city of Troy, he volunteered his services, and acted with the company until the cessation of hostilities. This company was among the first dispatched to the northern frontier, and was stationed at French Mill, now Fort Covington.

On the night of the 22d of October, 1812, Lieutenant Marcy accompanied a detachment under command of Major Young, whose object it was to capture a company of Canadian Militia posted at St. Regis. The attack was successful, and the whole force of the enemy were taken prisoners. The latter occupied a house built of heavy square timber, but though they were advantageously situated for defence, made only a feeble resistance. Lieutenant Marcy approached the house with a file of men, broke open the door himself at the hazard of his life, and after the garrison surrendered took from each man his arms. These were the first prisoners taken on land during the war. Among the spoils of the expedition was the flag of the British company, which was also the first standard taken on land. This flag was afterwards presented to Governor Tompkins, and is still preserved among the honored trophies of the war of 1812.

He was also with Colonel Pike and his regiment, in the unfortunate night expedition, in the month of November, against the British encampment on Le Colle River.

In 1816 he was appointed Recorder of the City of Troy, from which office he was removed in 1818, to give place to a supporter of Governor Clinton, whom he had voted for as the republican candidate for Governor, but with whose administration he had become dissatisfied, and which he had denounced as leaning too much towards the Federalists. In January, 1821, he received from Governor Yates the appointment of Adjutant-General of the New York State Militia; and in February, 1823, he was elected by the Legislature Comptroller of the State, to fill the vacancy occasioned by the appointment of John Savage to the Supreme Bench.

The duties of this office compelling his presence at the seat of government he removed to Albany, where he has since resided, excepting whilst engaged officially at Washington. In 1829, he was appointed one of the Associate Justices of the Supreme Court of the State of New York, but resigned that office on the 31st of January, 1831, at the urgent solicitation of his friends, upon his almost unanimous nomination as Senator by a legislative caucus, and on the following day was duly elected to the Senate of the United States.

He took his seat as Senator in December of that year, and remained in the Senate about two years, performing whilst there the duties of Chairman of the Committee on the Judiciary, and those pertaining to a Member of the Committee on Finance.

In 1832, Mr. Marcy was elected Governor of the State of New York, over Francis Granger, the Anti-Masonic candidate, by a majority of nearly ten thousand. His term as a Senator had not expired at the time of his election, but he resigned in season to enter upon his duties as Governor, on the first day of January, 1833. In his first message, he ably reviews the financial condition of the State, and thus expresses himself in regard to its indebtedness:

"A national debt may be the result of inevitable necessity. The efforts which nations are sometimes required to make, to recover their civil liberty, or to defend their rights, may involve an expenditure beyond their present ability to pay. A debt thus contracted confers no reproach, and its payment may be deferred until the people that incurred it, have replenished their resources, and become able to sustain the burden of discharging it, without withering their prosperity. Such has been the origin of our national debt, and such has been our course in regard to its payment. The debt contracted by this State on account of its canals, is justified on a different principle. The object for which it was incurred was specific, and ample means for its speedy redemption were provided in the very act which authorized it. It could have in no event been forwarded on to a future age, as an encumbrance upon it, to be paid by a general tax, without a violation of the most solemn pledges."

His views respecting the canals are thus given:

"There is no subject connected with our local affairs that we can contemplate with so much satisfaction as our works of internal improvement. The advantages resulting from them are felt in all parts of the state, and in the diversified occupations of our citizens. Everywhere their beneficial effects are visible, bearing testimony to the wisdom which conceived the system, and to the enterprise which put it into practical operation. The peculiar formation indicated at an early period to some of our enlightened and sagacious citizens, the practicability, as well as the usefulness of connecting the great northern and western lakes with the Atlantic ocean by means of artificial water communications. The enterprise of the present age has most successfully carried into effect the grand conceptions of the past. The spirit which prompted us to enter upon the system was not, however, wild and reckless; while it anxiously sought the end, it carefully estimated and wisely provided the means for its attainment. Though much has been done to improve the condition of our state, much yet remains to be done. While we allow the success which has attended our efforts at home to impel us forward in the career of improvement, we should not be regardless of the less fortunate efforts which have resulted from similar enterprises abroad. On the one hand, it would be unworthy of the character of the state to pause in this career; on the other, it would be more unwise to rush forward in it, accumulating burdens on the people without securing proportionate advantages."

Governor Marcy's administration had been so satisfactory that he was again nominated for re-election by the Herkimer Convention on the 10th of September, 1834, and defeated his opponent, Wm. H. Seward, by a majority of about thirteen thousand.

During his second term, in view of the strenuous efforts then being made by the State of Pennsylvania to divert the trade of the West through channels of its extensive lines of railroads and canals, Governor Marcy strongly urged upon the legislature the enlargement of the Erie Canal, but, true to the principles of his former message, he recommended that it should only be carried on as rapidly as the surplus revenues arising from tolls would permit.

Governor Marcy was nominated for a third term in 1836; and, to show his increasing popularity, we may add that he received at this election almost thirty thousand votes over the whig candidate, Jesse Buel.

Mr. Marcy was the candidate of the democratic party for a fourth term in 1838, but owing to causes which it is unnecessary for us to detail, he did not obtain his usual success, and Wm. H. Seward was elected governor.

After the expiration of his term of office, he was appointed by President Van Buren, one of the commissioners to decide upon the claims of the Mexican Government, under the convention of April, 1839. He performed the duties of this commission until its expiration in 1842, when he returned to Albany.

Upon the election of Mr. Polk to the Presidency, he tendered to Mr. Marcy the post of Secretary at War in his cabinet, which he accepted, and the arduous duties of which position he performed with signal ability during the late war with Mexico. It was the administration of this office that called forth the practical talents of Mr. Marcy. Upon him now devolved the very delicate duty of conducting a war, in regard to the prosecution of which Congress was by no means unanimous,—of appointing proper officers, and distributing *materiel* reluctantly granted by a divided representation. But his genius overcame all difficulties; and when the gallant generals and brave soldiers of those campaigns are named with the honors so justly merited, the services of the able secretary who watched over and guided their movements should not be forgotten.

Among the many drawbacks to the development of his plans, was an unfortunate feeling which had arisen to his prejudice in the bosoms of those gallant generals at the head of the separate columns in Mexico—a feeling, unhappily not unusual, where military men, and those whom they consider civilians, come in contact, particularly where the civilian has power to enforce his orders: and with General Scott especially, circumstances occurred to aggravate this feeling, forcing him to strictures upon the secretary, which doubtless in his calmer moments were regretted. Mr. Marcy defended himself with his usual ability, as the following extracts from a letter to General Scott will prove:—

"By extending my comments upon your letter, I might multiply proofs to show that your accusations against the head of the War Department are unjust; that your complaints are unfounded; that the designs imputed by you to the government to embarrass your operations, impair your rightful authority as commander, and to offer outrage and insult to your feelings, are all the mere creations of a distempered fancy; but to do more than I have done, would, in my judgment, be a work of supererogation.

"In conclusion, I may be permitted to say, that as one of the president's advisers, I had a *full share* in the *responsibility* of the act which assigned you to the command of our armies in Mexico. I felt interested, even more than naturally appertained to my official position, that success and glory should signalize your operations. It was my duty to bring to your aid the efficient co-operation of the war department. I never had a feeling that did not harmonize with a full and fair discharge of this duty. *I know it has been faithfully performed.*

"There are some men for whom enough cannot be done to make them grateful, or even just, unless acts of subserviency and personal devotedness are superadded. From you I expected bare justice, but have been disappointed. I have found you my accuser. In my vindication I have endeavored to maintain a defensive line, and if I have gone beyond it at any time, it has been done to repel unprovoked aggression. To your fame I have endeavored to be just. I have been gratified with the many occasions I have had to bear public testimony to your abilities and signal services as a commander in the field. It has been, and under any change in our personal relations, it will continue to be, my purpose to be liberal in my appreciation of your distinguished military merits. In respect to your errors and your faults, though I could not be blind, I regret that you have not permitted me to be silent."

Mr. Marcy was a prominent member of Mr. Polk's cabinet, and apart from the services intimately connected with his position as secretary of war, exerted no small influence upon the other questions which came before it. His diplomacy was displayed in the settlement of the Oregon boundary. He was an advocate of the tariff of 1846: and always advised a strict adherence to the old democratic doctrine of protecting the states in all their rights which did not conflict with the federal constitution. On the slavery question, especially, was he decided that interference was not only pernicious, but unconstitutional.

In the presidential election of 1848, he supported General Cass; and when General Taylor was elected, he retired at the expiration of Mr. Polk's term to his home at Albany, where he remained a useful and an active citizen, until the election of Mr. Pierce, who tendered him the office of secretary of state, which he now fills with such distinguished ability.

Mr. Pierce, in his inaugural, having assumed a position in regard to the rights of American citizens abroad, which found a ready response in the bosoms of all who claimed protection under our flag, whether native or adopted, an opportunity not long since presented itself of testing the applicability of his views; and as the matter came directly under the action of the secretary of state, to the diplomatic talents of Mr. Marcy may be attributed the conducting of those cabinet measures upon the protest of Chevalier Hulsemann, in behalf of the Austrian government; and to his statesmanship the masterly vindication of President Pierce's inaugural, and the conduct of the officers of the American government, as displayed in the Koszta correspondence.

Near the close of the month of July, 1853, Martin Koszta, a Hungarian by birth, but clothed with the nationality of the United States by a previous legal declaration of his intention to become a citizen, was set upon by a gang of villains in the port of Smyrna, and finally carried on board of an Austrian vessel, where he was detained in irons as a traitor to the Austrian government. Mr. Brown, the dragoman of the American legation, having become aware of the facts, directed Capt. Ingraham, commander of the U. S. ship-of-war St. Louis, to demand the surrender of Koszta and to employ force, if necessary, to compel a compliance with his application. The Austrian legation yielded to the superior power, under protest, and upon condition that Koszta should be placed in the custody of the French legation, and be delivered up only upon the written consent both of the American and Austrian ministers.

Almost simultaneously with the receipt of this news in the United States, Chevalier Hulsemann, Chargé of the Austrian Government, addressed the Secretary of State a note protesting on behalf of his government against the action of Mr. Brown, and of Capt. Ingraham, and asking our government to authorize the surrender of Koszta to the Austrian government.

As the first important measure of public policy which the present administration has had an opportunity of submitting to the world, this letter of Mr. Marcy has naturally attracted very general attention, aside from the profound interest felt in the question to which it relates. It can well bear all the scrutiny to which it may be subjected. It is universally admitted to be one of the ablest state papers that ever emanated from Washington. It has covered its author and his country with new honor, and will inspire the whole civilized world with increased respect for American statesmanship and the American flag. It has disposed of the Koszta controversy. It is conceded to be a perfect vindication of Mr. Brown and of Capt. Ingraham as for the orders of the one and their faithful and manly execution by the other, and henceforth no one will presume to deny that in the Ottoman empire, all who have clothed themselves with the nationality of our government, are entitled to and will receive its protection.

As a private citizen Governor Marcy has always been held in high esteem, for his good example in the fulfilment of social duties and obligations, for his public spirit, and for his generous liberality.

In person he is rather above the ordinary height; his frame is stout and muscular, but not gross. His forehead is bold and full; his eyebrows heavy; his eyes deep-set and expressive; and his mouth and chin firmly moulded. His appearance altogether is calculated to impress a stranger favorably, both in respect to his talents and his character. His manners are affable and courteous; free from pretence, yet dignified. His acquaintance is really an enjoyment, and he is one of those men to whom society is indebted for its charms and attractions.

He is considered to be a strict party man, but frank and honorable in his political course. He has the reputation of being a shrewd political tactician, and, probably, has never been surpassed in this respect, by any of the politicians of New York. It has ever been his policy to prevent the getting up of State issues to interfere with the success of the democratic party of the nation. He is something of an optimist in politics, regarding everything as for the best, never disturbed by reverses, nor unduly elated by good fortune. He is well fitted, too, to *rough it*,—a desirable trait in a politician, for he has his dark days as well as sunshine.

As a writer, he ranks high. His style is strong, pure, perspicuous, and flows with true Addisonian ease and elegance. His state papers are admirable compositions of their kind, and, like those of Clarendon and Bolingbroke, will be remembered for their intrinsic worth, long after the subjects to which they relate have lost their importance.

Secretary Marcy has been twice married. His first wife was a Miss Newell, a descendant of one of the early settlers of Sturbridge; his second was a daughter of the late Benjamin Knower, of the city of Albany, at one time State Treasurer.

It would not be easy to find a man who possesses a greater amount of general information than Secretary Marcy. He seems to be as familiar with every department of science and literature as if his life had been spent in their pursuit. His insatiable thirst for knowledge has been constantly gratified and stimulated by new acquisitions; while an iron constitution, which has shown itself proof against any amount of intellectual exertion, has enabled him to push his researches, without interruption, to the present hour. What he thus acquires seems always at perfect command. There is no confusion in his knowledge. His mind is like a well ordered cabinet, where everything is skilfully arranged and available; where every shell, and gem, and fossil, and mineral, is within reach, either for ornament or illustration.

His memory is very remarkable: it is, perhaps, one of the secrets of his strength, as it certainly forms a considerable source of the fascination of his conversation. He is a man of vivid impressions. What he hears and what he reads, no less than what he sees, seems to be daguerreotyped upon his mind, never to fade. He has as clear a conception of the stirring events which have taken place within the last fifty years, in both hemispheres, as if they had passed under his own eye. Persons distinguished in our own history, now long dead, with whom he has had intercourse, are as distinctly remembered as if he had parted with them but yesterday. Racy anecdotes, illustrative of their characters and of their times, and therefore matters of general interest, are told by him with all the freshness of a recent occurrence. As with an enchanter's wand, he raises the curtain, and exhibits past events, making them, like well executed tableaux, to stand out as present realities. It is on such occasions that the regret is often repeated, that he does not employ his gifted pen in delineating interesting reminiscences, which will otherwise die with him.

As an extemporaneous speaker, he stands deservedly high. His manner is calm, deliberate, dignified, graceful, and impressive. The same classic elegance and chasteness of language which belong to his written opinions, also characterize his extemporaneous addresses. It was a common remark, that his language could not be improved, but was ready for the press just as it fell from his lips. The author remembers one occasion when, under the influence of strong emotion, he spoke for two hours, with a sustained and thrilling and masterly eloquence that he has never seen surpassed. The smoothly flowing stream had become a torrent, that swept on with a resistless momentum. He was cool, cautious, and ready; presenting the strongest points of his client's cause in the most winning and advantageous aspects; and defending, with admirable skill, those which were more assailable. No man could parry better than he the force of an adverse authority, or show greater ingenuity in discriminating his case from the one cited against him.

The writer would do injustice to the subject of this sketch, did he neglect to speak particularly of those social qualities, which constitute one of the most attractive features of his character. He shines in the department of domestic and social life. It is in the unreserved intercourse which mutual love and esteem produce, that the charm of his conversation is felt by both young and old. It is here that his real amiability of disposition finds full play. With a lively and cultivated imagination; a ready, genial wit, which pleases all without wounding any; quickness at repartee; an inexhaustible fund of anecdote, relating to matters and things and persons, within his own recollection; great general information and power of graphic delineation; all united with the manners and bearing of a thorough gentleman, render him at once the ornament, as well as the favorite of social life. An evening spent with him, when he is in one of his best colloquial moods, is an event to be remembered.

Mr. Marcy is now near the age of three-score years and ten, in possession of full bodily and mental vigor; with an eye as keen and as full of fire as in his younger days. He is still actively engaged in the acquisition of useful knowledge, and in keeping up with the progress of the age; performing an amount of labor and reading, that many younger men would regard as no inconsiderable task. He looks with eager interest upon the panorama of this moving world, allowing no item of general interest in any part of the globe to escape him.

Engd. by H.B. Hall.

James Guthrie

SECRETARY OF THE UNITED STATES TREASURY

Engd. for Biographical Sketches of Eminent American Lawyers

JAMES GUTHRIE,

SECRETARY OF THE TREASURY.

James Guthrie, Secretary of the Treasury, was born in Nelson County, state of Kentucky, in the year 1793, and is now sixty years of age. Though not of Scotch parentage, he is of Scotch descent, his ancestors having emigrated first from Scotland to Ireland, and afterwards to this country. Guthrie is a name well and advantageously known in Scottish history. It was James Guthrie, a Covenanting minister who, for his intrepidity as a preacher and writer, was marked for a victim, by the perfidious government of Charles the Second. He was condemned to death as a traitor with no other solemnity than the form of a trial, and was soon afterwards executed. He met his death (by decapitation) heroically, and from the scaffold exhorted the numerous spectators to resist the tyrant and persecutor to the death. Then having done, with as much tranquillity as if he had been in his pulpit, he submitted his neck to the executioner's axe. His head was placed over a gateway in Edinburgh, and was regarded by the persecuted covenanters as an object of peculiar reverence. To him and to such as he was, Scotland owes her religious liberty—a debt never to be forgotten.

Mr. Guthrie's father was General Adam Guthrie, an early pioneer to the west from the state of Virginia. He was an active, energetic man, and bore a distinguished part in the struggle with the Indians for that flourishing region, now composing six or seven states and numbering five or six millions of inhabitants. It was then an unexplored, inhospitable wilderness. What will it be one hundred years hence? General Guthrie, besides being engaged in other conflicts with the Indians, was in the battle of the Saline, fought ten or twelve miles west of Shawnee town, Illinois, and which was remarkable for the singular manner in which it was gained by the whites—by charging with the tomahawk (they had no bayonets) through the Indian line, and after breaking it charging to the right and left. In this engagement, General William Hardin, the commander of the expedition, was seriously wounded.

Peace being made with the Indians, General Guthrie turned his attention wholly to civil pursuits, and became so far a politician as to represent his county in the Kentucky Legislature eight or ten years, to the entire satisfaction of his constituents and of his fellow citizens in general. He was a man of strong practical sense, and was much esteemed for that, as well as for the fidelity with which he adhered to friendships formed in the hour of trial and danger.

James Guthrie was educated principally at McAlister's Academy at Bardstown in Nelson county, an institution which was at that day one of the best to be found in the western country. The head of it was a Scotchman, and by no means an ordinary man. He was distinguished for his general attainments and for his extensive mathematical knowledge, and esteemed and beloved for the urbanity of his manners, and the benevolence of his disposition. Having completed his academical course, Mr.

Guthrie, as it was then common for active and adventurous young men to do, engaged in the Mississippi trade, purchasing the produce of his neighborhood, and descending the river with it in that grotesque-looking and forgotten craft, called a *Flat*. Whilst engaged in this pursuit he thrice visited New Orleans, returning home on horseback or on foot. through the Indian country; to do which was no small undertaking, as it required both mental resolution and physical strength. There were great pedestrians engaged in that trade in those days, whose feats of walking were even then marvellous, and in these more soft and silken times almost incredible. There were men who performed, on foot, the land journey of eight or nine hundred miles, sooner than it could be accomplished by any horseman; and as many as thirty such journeys have been performed by a single individual.

Finding the business of a river trader a very laborious and hazardous one, and not very remunerative, Mr. Guthrie abandoned it and returned to the study of the law, which he had once before commenced and now resumed, after an intermission of a year or two, under the instruction of the late Judge Rowan, a profound jurist and eloquent advocate. The judge was an able man, who won his way to political and forensic distinction by his talents, tact, and energy. He was often a member of the Legislature of his own state, and was six years a Senator of the United States.

Mr. Guthrie was at this period a severe student—retired and taciturn—not mingling with society in its pleasure, or feeding his mind upon the idle and transient topics of gossip too often discussed in circles of the young and giddy—but in laborious study over the works of the sages of the law. He criticisised, assimilated, and digested the matter of his reading, until he made it his own. He knew that it was only in the study of the law as a science that its symmetry could be discerned, and its adaptation to its ends fully appreciated; and that he who is a mere case lawyer, is driven at every turn to resort to his books, could neither illustrate its great principles, nor apply them with skill to the multiform cases that arise in practice.

In 1820, Mr. Guthrie established himself as a practitioner of law in the town, now city, of Louisville, and soon became eminent in his profession. He possessed the qualities and qualifications that command success, and he commanded it. With a vigorous intellect, much legal knowledge, and great industry, he secured in a very short time a large share of the most lucrative practice. No man ever approached him as a client who did not want a strictly conscientious adviser or advocate. He never gave "forked counsel," and always regarded the law, not as a trade full of trickery and tergiversation, but as a noble science, the professors of which ought, in their professional capacity, to be as spotless as the ermine of that justice whose guardians and administrators they are. By his practice he acquired in a few years means enough, when under the management of his prudence and discernment, to lay the foundation of a large fortune, which he did, not by what are called "lucky hits," and which are no more than fortunate accidents—for he is no visionary or reckless speculator—but by judicious investments in real estate in and around Louisville, the future greatly enhanced value of which he clearly foresaw, aad much more distinctly than many others who occupied themselves entirely in speculation.

Though assiduously devoted to his profession, Mr. Guthrie found time to participate in the political questions by which the state of Kentucky was so portentously agitated for some seven or eight years, dating from about the year 1821. Party animosity scarcely ever before ran so high in this country, and the exasperation and violence could hardly have been greater, stopping short of civil war. This state of things grew out of what were called the relief measures, adopted by the legislature—stay and replevin laws, in connexion with the commonwealth's bank, and the reorganization of the court of appeals. Mr. Guthrie was opposed in principle to any interference of the legislature in a question between debtor and creditor, but believing that it had the unquestionable power to remodel its judicature, he was on the side of the new court against the old, and was one of the ablest and most adroit defenders of the cause he espoused. The old court party finally succeeded, but their success did not settle definitively any of the questions at issue. What seemed to be a final adjustment of them was but an adjournment, for they may, under a parity of circumstances, be again asserted and again contended for by another generation on the same arena.

Of all those relief measures the commonwealth's bank was perhaps the boldest experiment, and was as successful as it was bold. Nothing of the kind has ever been attempted in this country and been so successfully carried through. Three millions of paper dollars were put into circulation without any metallic basis whatever, and with no capital except the public faith; and after doing good service to the country, saving thousands of debtors from ruin, and materially aiding to support the government of the state, the whole was in few years called in, cancelled, and destroyed. It is doubtful whether such a public-financial achievement could be again accomplished in Kentucky, or in any other country. Ten millions of dollars would be no more for that state now than three millions were then, but certainly no statesman of that commonwealth would be willing to see so large a sum emitted except upon a specie basis large enough to constitute a reasonable guarantee for its final redemption.

Mr. Guthrie has often represented the city of Louisville and the county of Jefferson in the legislature of his own state, first in the lower house and afterwards in the senate, and he has been almost always elected with a majority against him, with respect to political opinion; but such was the confidence reposed in his ability and integrity, and in his zeal for the general good, that many of his opponents preferred him to candidates from among their own party. This was a high compliment, and in his case a most deserved one. In the legislature he was generally chairman of the judiciary committee, and he discharged his duties as such with great industry and intelligence. He rarely ever proposed a measure respecting the state tribunals which was not sanctioned, for he never proposed anything that was not a manifest amelioration. Though far from being a loquacious member, he was not by any means a silent one, but spoke frequently for or against propositions as they came up, and spoke always clearly, forcibly, and convincingly. He is not in the slightest degree what Hazlitt says Canning was—"a mere fluent sophist," or what Goldsmith said of Burke, addicted to "refining," and to "cutting blocks with a razor." His speeches were all to the purpose, and whilst they were lucid and perspicuous, were not much embellished by the mere graces and polish of elocution. They needed no such embellishment. Mr. Guthrie's aim was to be clear, brief, logical, and precise, without much regarding rhetorical ornament and appliances. He was not considered a great orator, but was looked upon as being something much more useful and influential in a deliberative body—a great debater and great business man, and was for that reason always listened to with the most profound attention by all parties.

It has been frequently asked: "Why has not Mr. Guthrie had a greater reputation out of his own state?" A very short sentence will fully answer the question. He has no political ambition. Often has he been solicited, nay, importuned, to become a candidate for the gubernatorial chair of the state, and for Congress, and as often has he positively declined the invitation. Without doubt he might have been in the councils of the nation, where the same qualities which have made him eminent at home would have secured him distinction in a more elevated position. His fondness for politics begins and ends in his patriotism. He covets no fame, no office, nor the emoluments of office. He has not been a seeker after popularity, and all he has enjoyed has been of the kind which Lord Mansfield said was alone worth having—that which follows and is not sought. He is zealous and untiring in the advocacy of sound political principles, but from choice has limited his sphere of action to his own county and state. From 1825 to the present day, he has been what many would call a Jackson democrat, and a most active, influential, and efficient one. To his exertions his party is much indebted for the formidable and imposing front the Democrats have always presented to their antagonists in Kentucky, although almost constantly in the minority; and though he has left the state temporarily, it is not likely that his example and his efforts will be forgotten. He will not now interfere in the state politics; but his past labors will not be lost, for many choice spirits still remain to imitate and to emulate his devotedness and disinterestedness.

In the formation of his Cabinet, President Pierce wished to place at the head of the Treasury a man of tried principles, and of acknowledged qualifications. Such a man was Mr. Guthrie; but yet upon a question or two of national policy, his sentiments were not quite as familiar to the President as the latter wished; not that there was anything covert or ambiguous about Mr. Guthrie with respect to his opinions, but what was perfectly well known in Kentucky was not so well known in New Hampshire; and for that reason he was indirectly interrogated upon those points. His answer was characteristic—brief, pointed, and unequivocal. Instead of treating the subject diffusely, and writing a dissertation, he did but little more than refer, for full information, to the speeches he had made in the Kentucky Convention which formed a new constitution for that state, some three or four years ago, and of which body he was the President. But so little value did he seem to place upon his parliamentary labors that he had not preserved even a copy of those speeches, and merely said, they would be found in the debates of that Convention. These speeches furnished the information desired by the President, and added greatly to his reputation as a statesman and debater. In that body he not only performed the duties of presiding officer in a most dignified and satisfactory manner, but was at the same time an active, enlightened, and influential member, whose opinions upon every important point were eagerly listened to and almost invariably adopted.

It may be said, and cannot be contradicted, that as Secretary of the Treasury no one has ever had the charge of that Department, who has brought more industry, integrity, and ability to the performance of his duties than Mr. Guthrie; and no Secretary, in so short a time, ever more completely mastered the details of the office or made himself more intimately acquainted with the fiscal and commercial system of the country. Strict economy, a strict adherence to the laws, and strict accountability, form the basis of his administrative system, and should he remain in office until the 4th of March, 1857, and meet with that cöoperation and support which it may be confidently assumed he will, the fiscal affairs of the country will be in a condition to challenge the admiration, as they will excite the envy, of all the governments of Europe; for a triumph will have been achieved by the "great republic" more glorious than the winning of a dozen battles, if not so dazzling. The 4th of March, 1857, will be the second time within the memory of man, when a heavy public debt will have been entirely paid off, and the nation once more relieved from that very equivocal "national blessing," a national debt. *Then* we shall have no pecuniary liabilities, a full treasury, and imposts that will not be much more than nominal, and will move on with accelerated speed in our career of prosperity and progress.

The character of Mr. Guthrie's mind is eminently inductive and analytical; there is nothing about it startling or electrical. Slow and cautious, even to fastidiousness, in his premises, he reaches his conclusions with the most painstaking accuracy. His "fancy is tame," and it may be truly said of it, that it "waits upon the judgment." He never contents himself with brilliant analogies, so apt to captivate the undisciplined mind. For himself he digs into the mine of truth, and makes no account of the reputation often gained by a mere brokerage in the precious ore. He recognises no authority but that which carries with it its own inherent sanction. He measures the shoals and depths of his subject with the line and plummet of reason, and if ever man was, is willing to follow her behests, "uncaring consequences."

As a speaker, he is impassioned, with a warmth of earnest conviction felt by himself, and desired to be instilled into his auditors. He employs no ornaments of speech, but few anecdotes, indulges in no play of fancy, and never aims to direct his hearers from his subject to himself or his style. His speech is direct, earnest, and for a result—addressed more to the understanding than the passions. His earnestness and self-conviction, his steady array and disciplined precision of thought, with his frequent recurrence to great and familiar principles, and their application, all combined, effect all that the most eloquent could accomplish.

In addition to his qualifications as an advocate, he has a clear and instinctive perception, and appreciation of the universal principles of justice and right; and as an equity lawyer, has few equals. Throughout his entire professional career, he has ever manifested a singular devotion to the interests of his clients. He always made their cause his own when founded in justice, and lent the whole energies of his mind to sustain it. He enjoyed the unlimited confidence of all who have sought his services, and his sincerity and integrity were never even the subject of suspicion or distrust. The poor, when oppressed, or deprived of a right, have never appealed to him without meeting with sympathy and aid; and he has freely bestowed, not only his time and professional services, but often advanced his money to assist a feeble and helpless client. Indeed, this class of his business has always been remarkably large, yet it has been cheerfully performed, and usually attended with most gratifying success.

In all his varied fortunes, he has never seemed for one moment to forget the associates of his early life. His sympathies are with the *people*, who have been his fast and unyielding friends, and have ever been his chief reliance in all the sterner trials of his life. They have clung to him in every period of his fortunes, with a devotion that no circumstances could weaken, nor adversity overcome. Ever ready to aid them with his counsel, his advice, his sympathy, and assistance, he has found in them in return, on all occasions where their efforts were required to sustain him in the discharge of his public duties, a support upon which he has relied with unfailing confidence, and to which he never made an appeal in vain. Regardless of mere wealth and empty distinction, he seldom sought the aid or association of those whose energies were exclusively devoted to the accumulation of riches, and never had the fortune to count this class in the ranks of his ardent personal friends. He was drawn instinctively into communion with those whose lot it is to toil, endure, and suffer, and found his chief enjoyment in the society of those honest and humble men, who in the seclusion of private life remained free from the corruptions of wealth, and the debasing tendencies of unscrupulous personal ambition.

A great and leading trait of his character is a benevolence of feeling. From the first hour of his prosperity, he has freely shared the avails of his labors with his kindred, many of whom required the aid of some friendly hand to raise them from the same condition of poverty and toil in which his own lot was cast, and scarcely a day passes by but some friend is permitted to share his bounty.

The great element in his success has been an iron will and unyielding perseverance. In the darkest hour of his life, when adversity pressed most heavily upon him, he never for a moment gave way to despair, or relaxed the energies of his ardent and hopeful nature. He commenced the great battle of life resolved to conquer and overcome, and the results he has been able to accomplish, over the opposing forces that beset him, show how well and how wisely he has maintained the contest.

In his history, no man can fail to find encouragement. The most formidable obstacles yield to the force of a steady determination, and often when least expected, the resolute heart finds in the lessons of its own experience, the truth of that beautiful Irish expression, "*there is a silver lining to every cloud.*"

The tendency of his duties and studies has been to purify, and elevate, and strengthen the moral sense; and to inspire respect and reverence for those immutable moral principles, which are essential to the welfare of man and the peace of society. Purity of life, in every relation, is of prime importance in the character of a public man. Without it, genius, learning, wit, eloquence, and cultivation, are worse than in vain. They add only to the length of the lever by which vice dissolves the fabric of individual character and social welfare. And we conceive it to be the highest eulogium we can bestow upon Mr. Guthrie, to say that he is a pure man.

A scholar he is, and a ripe one, too, but he is not a learned man in the common acceptation of the phrase. He has dropped the speculative sciences long since, and given his mind only to those practical pursuits which in a country like ours are so much more useful. His quick perceptions make him a man of true sagacity; his ardent temperament has given uncommon energy to his character, and his clear reason has purified his tastes, and made his judgment, though certainly not infallible, yet in the main altogether reliable.

But the strong hold he has on the affections of his friends, is better accounted for by his attractive social and moral qualities. The unselfish and generous impulses of his nature do not permit him to serve any one by halves, and yet his opponents have never had cause to complain that his demeanor towards them was wanting either in justice or in courtesy. Sincerity, that first of virtues, is the characteristic trait of his mind. His whole conduct is full of transparent truthfulness. His speeches are marked with a sort of daring plainness. Concealment of his opinions, whatever may be the effect of their utterance upon himself or others, seems with him to be out of the question.

> His heart's his mouth.
> What his breast forges, that his tongue must vent.
> He would not flatter Neptune for his trident,
> Or Jove for his power to thunder.

It may be that Mr. Guthrie will retire, after the close of the present administration, to private life. At all events, it is impossible now to predict whether higher honors await him or not. But no matter what may be his future career, he has already earned the title of an able lawyer, an incorruptible public servant, and an honest man. Of such a character it is fit that the dignity should be vindicated and the value made known.

As a father our subject is most affectionate and devoted. His family constitute an object most dear to his heart; and a desire to advance the happiness and comfort of his two daughters is a paramount feeling. When not forced abroad in the discharge of public duties, his own fireside forms the point of attraction, where he can always be found. With a warm heart and generous impulses, he is the centre of a circle of devoted friends. His social qualities are very great. Possessed of fine colloquial powers, he never fails to make himself both instructive and interesting as a companion; and always dignified in deportment, yet he is easy of access, and especially affable to the young.

In closing this brief memoir, the remark seems to be called for, that the incidents which it records, may not be altogether useless as presenting for consideration the notice of one who, in defiance of seemingly adverse circumstances in early life, has risen to stations of official prominence and responsibility. Our country, under the benign influence of her admirable republican institutions, has furnished many such instances; and it is certainly meet that all such should have an enduring record, if for no other purpose than to encourage others, under similar disadvantages, to struggle manfully and hopefully with the difficulties which they are called to encounter.

Here ends this brief notice of Mr. Guthrie, which cannot be very satisfactory to those who are desirous of knowing much about the able and energetic head of the Treasury Department. To write anything like a minute biographical notice of him would require more time and space than can now be given to the subject; and such a notice would comprise in a great measure a political and forensic history of the State of Kentucky for the last quarter of a century.

J C Dobbin

OF NORTH CAROLINA,
SECRETARY OF THE UNITED STATES NAVY.

Engraved for Biographical Sketches of Eminent Americans.

HON JAMES C. DOBBIN

SECRETARY OF THE NAVY,

Is a native of Fayetteville, North Carolina, and the eldest child of John M. and Ahness C. Dobbin. He was born in 1814, and named after his maternal grandfather, James Cochrane, who represented the Orange district in Congress during the war of 1812.

His father, John M. Dobbin, was a merchant in Fayetteville during a period of thirty years, and died in 1837, universally regretted.

At an early age the subject of this memoir was sent to school in his native town, where he rapidly acquired the rudiments of a classical education. Afterwards he was sent by his father to the school of Mr. W. J. Bingham, in Hillsboro', N. C., where he was prepared for college. In 1828 he entered the freshman class of the University of North Carolina, when he was about fourteen years old.

At the University he was distinguished for a prompt and faithful discharge of every duty imposed upon him, as also for a ready and cheerful observance of all the rules and regulations of that institution. He was considerably the youngest member in his class, and for four years manfully sustained himself and boldly took his stand among the foremost in that honorable field of rivalry, and in 1832 graduated with high distinction in the same class with Hon. Thomas L. Clingman, John H. Haughton and Thomas S. Ashe, Esquires, and other distinguished gentlemen. Throughout his entire college course Mr. Dobbin was a universal favorite with the students and faculty at Chapel Hill, and so far had his amiable traits of character won upon the affections of the venerable president, Dr. Caldwell, that he has been heard to say in the bosom of his family: " It would gladden his heart to be the father of such a son as James C. Dobbin."

After graduating, Mr. Dobbin commenced the study of law in the office of the Hon. Robert Strange, at that time one of the judges who presided on the Superior Court Bench, in North Carolina, and under his guidance and instruction, devoted two and a half years to the *mastery* of that science which has been denominated the " perfection of reason."

During a portion of the time that Mr. Dobbin read law with Judge Strange he was also an inmate of his house and a member of his family, and thus possessed the advantage of the judge's oral instruction during leisure hours, and also laid the foundation of that reciprocal affection and esteem that have so increased upon them until long since the distinctions of teacher and pupil have passed away, or rather have been merged in those of fond companions and bosom friends.

In 1835, Mr. Dobbin, having read well and closely Coke on Littleton, Blackstone's Commentaries, Chitty's Pleading, Starkie on Evidence, and such other books as his preceptor had prescribed, and having now attained his majority, he applied for and obtained his license to practise law. He immediately opened a law office in Fayetteville, N. C., and most assiduously devoted himself to a strict and regular attendance at it. During office hours, whether clients came or not, he was always *in* his office, and this regularity of custom in a short time had considerable influence upon his professional success.

Mr. Dobbin did not, as too many young lawyers do, select an extensive circuit in the outset, but wisely husbanded his time and energies for a faithful discharge of chamber business in Fayetteville, and in attendance upon the County and Superior Courts of Cumberland, Robeson and Sampson. His theory was and still is, "Let a man build up a reputation at home, let it radiate and precede him rather than that he should precede it." Upon this theory he has always acted, and every extension of his circuit has more resembled a triumph than an effort to succeed.

The first capital case in which Mr. Dobbin appeared was, where one negro man was indicted in Cumberland Superior Court, in 1837, for the murder of another negro. He had the honor to be associated in the defence, with the Hon. Robert Strange, who had just been elected U. S. Senator, and had resigned his seat upon the bench. In the management of the defence, Mr. Dobbin displayed great subtlety and ingenuity, and in his arguments to the jury, gave evidence of those peculiar talents that have since ranked him with the most successful and ablest criminal advocates in North Carolina. Throughout the range of our acquaintance we know of no lawyer's history that is more instructive and encouraging to young members of the profession than that of Mr. Dobbin. No accidental circumstance occurred by which he seized on fame by a single effort. No one case can be cited as that which made the man. On the contrary, his practice and reputation have daily increased by a faithful and able discharge of duty. In his early career, too, "he was content to labor and to wait," and not ashamed to learn from such luminaries as Toomer Eccles, Strange and Henry, who were the leaders at the Fayetteville bar at the time of his admission, but with whom he was so shortly to contend.

He was frequently desired to represent his native county—Cumberland—in the state legislature, but this honor he invariably declined, alleging that he was happy and contented in the discharge of his professional duties, and conceived that he experienced more real joy in the bosom of his family than he could ever expect from the excitement of political life. To this determination he adhered until 1845, when the democratic party nominated him as a candidate to represent them in Congress, from the Raleigh district. The nomination was unsought and unexpected, and taking into account his youth, his retired life, the district, and the able men who resided in it, he could not regard it as otherwise than an extremely flattering testimonial of the high estimation in which he was held, and after some hesitation he accepted the nomination, and entered upon the campaign. His competitor was his old class-mate, John H. Haughton, Esq., an able and talented whig. At the close of the campaign, however, Mr. Dobbin was ascertained to be elected by a majority of two thousand votes, whilst in the previous campaign his democratic predecessor had only beaten *his* whig rival about three hundred votes.

At the commencement of the 29th Congress, Mr. Dobbin was present and had the honor to be placed upon the committee on contested elections, and took a very active part in all its deliberations and reports.

In the contested election from Florida, between Cabell and Brockenbrough, Mr. Dobbin was of opinion Cabell was not entitled to his seat, and so voted.

In the New-Jersey contested election between Runk and Farlee, he was chairman of the majority committee, and submitted its report. In this case he was active and zealous, and labored hard to have the cause terminated at an early day. For having satisfied himself that nineteen of the students at the college in New-Jersey had a right to vote, he was anxious that justice should be done, by declaring that Farlee, democrat, was not entitled to his seat, but that Runk, the whig member, was—and his view of the case was finally sustained by a majority of the House.

On the Oregon question Mr. Dobbin spoke. He thought the time "for masterly inactivity" had gone by, and he was in favor of serving a notice on Great Britain to terminate the joint tenancy.

On the public land bill, then before Congress, he delivered an able and eloquent speech. He rose above party trammels, and said, "I am *opposed* to the policy of *ceding these lands to the states in which they lie*"—that neither justice nor any other consideration of sound policy required it, and appealed to gentlemen to strike that feature from the bill.

In this speech he advocated the necessity of striking from the statute book the tariff act of 1842, and after an elaborate argument, tending to prove that it taxed every other branch of industry, for the sole purpose of enriching the manufacturer, he proceeded to enforce his positions by a reference to the conduct of England, in the following beautiful and characteristic remarks :

"Mr. Chairman, it has fallen to our lot to become actors on the theatre of public life at a most remarkable era in the history of the world. The human mind, evincing its mighty and mysterious capabilities, is achieving triumphs at once wonderful and sublime. The elements of nature are playthings for it to sport with. Earth, ocean, air, lightning, yield subservient in the hands of genius, to minister to the wants, the purposes, and the pleasures of man. Science is fast developing to the meanest capacity the hidden secrets of nature, hitherto unexplored in the researches of philosophy. Education is exerting its mild and refining influences to elevate and bless the people. The control of electricity is astonishing the world. The power of steam is annihilating distance, and making remote cities and towns and strangers at once neighbors and friends. Amid these mighty movements in the fields of science, literature, and philosophy, the liberal spirit of free government, in its steady and onward progress, is beginning to accomplish much for the amelioration of the condition of the human family, so long the hope of the statesman and the philanthropist. The illiberal maxims of bad government—too long supported from false reverence for their antiquity—are beginning to give place to the enlightened suggestions of experience. England, the birthplace, is proposing to become the grave, of commercial restriction. In that land, whose political doctrines are so often the theme of our denunciation and satire, with all the artillery of landed aristocracy, associated wealth, and party vindictiveness leveled at him, there has appeared on the stage a learned, a leading premier, Sir Robert Peel, who, blending in his character much of the philosophy of Burke, the bold and matchless eloquence of Chatham, and the patriotism of Hampden, has had the moral courage and magnanimity to proclaim that he can no longer resist the convictions of experience and observation, and that the system of commercial restriction and high protection is wrong, oppressive, and should be abandoned. Already, sir, has much been done; already has the British tariff, so long pleaded as the excuse for ours, been radically reformed, and in obedience to the persevering demand of an outraged people, we hope that the next gale that crosses the Atlantic will come laden with the glorious tidings of a still greater triumph in the repeal of the corn laws, so oppressive to Englishmen and injurious to Americans.

"And shall we not reciprocate this liberal spirit? Shall republican America, so boastful of her greatness and freedom, be outstripped in her career in this cause of human rights by monarchical England? No, sir—I do not, cannot, and will not believe it. I have an abiding, unshaken faith in the ultimate triumph of so righteous a cause. Mr. Chairman, we may surpass the nations of the earth in science, in arms, and in arts; the genius of our people may attract the admiration of mankind—may cause 'beauty and symmetry to live on canvas'—may almost make the 'marble from the quarry to breathe and speak'—may charm the world with elegant attainments in poetry and learning—but much, very much will be unaccomplished; the beauty of our political escutcheon will still be marred while commerce is trammeled, and agriculture and trade depressed by bad legislation."

At the close of the session he returned to Fayetteville and prosecuted his legal pursuits with energy and zeal.

On the meeting of Congress, he was again in attendance, and on the "three million" bill he delivered a speech, which in its range embraced the "Mexican war," the "Wilmot Proviso," and the "extension of slave territory," that attracted the attention of the whole country, and ranked Mr. Dobbin among the ablest debaters in congress.

From this speech, which was much praised at the time as an able vindication of southern rights and interests upon constitutional grounds, and in a national spirit, we take the liberty of selecting, at random, some detached passages, as illustrative of his power of investing the most obstruse subjects with a graceful and peculiar charm.

"Mr. Dobbin next addressed the committee as follows:

"Mr. Chairman,—I do not rise upon this occasion for the purpose of republishing another edition of the history of the Mexican war. Its origin, its rise, and its progress, are familiar to the humblest cottager of the country as well as the most active politician in the capital. The fame of those gallant soldiers who fought and achieved the brilliant victories of Monterey and Resaca de la Palma, has crossed the confines of our own republic, and has elicited the applause and admiration of the mightiest powers on earth.

"But, Mr. Chairman, there *is* a war of recent origin, upon the origin, the rise, and the progress of which, I do propose to make some remarks this morning: I mean the war recently waged upon the reputation, the constitutional rights and domestic institutions of the southern states.

"Before I proceed, then, Mr. Chairman, to reply to the arguments used by these gentlemen, I take the liberty of doing what I regret these gentlemen did not do, of making, at least, *a respectful allusion to the constitution.* I have always thought, sir, it was the pride and boast of Americans that we not only lived in the enjoyment of the blessings of a free government, but that our rights, our property, and happiness, are protected by a *written constitution*, which we are all taught to regard as sacred and inviolable ; a constitution written by the *same* hands that had just wielded the sword in the cause of human freedom ; a constitution dictated by hearts burning with an ardent love of liberty, and just released from the thraldom of tyranny. And when a wise legislator—one who appreciates his responsibility as a representative, and his rights as a citizen—is invited into a new field of legislation, he turns to the pages of the constitution to learn whether he has the constitutional right to act, before he proceeds to the subordinate considerations of policy and expediency. And, sir, if there ever was a question which should call into exercise all our self-control, all our wisdom, all our patriotism, and a strict adherence to the constitution, it is this question of slavery—this dangerous rock upon which wise and good men have gloomily foreboded that our ship of state would one day be wrecked, and the world be called sadly to gaze upon the sundered and bleeding fragments of our once glorious and happy Union.

"But if we are true upon this occasion to ourselves—true to that constitution, the sheet-anchor of our safety—this storm-cloud that now darkens our political horizon, and threatens to break in its fury and scatter desolation and dismay through our wide-spread republic, will pass off in harmless silence, and leave behind it a clearer sky and a more genial sunshine. Sir, however exalted may be the patriotism, however honest the motives, however disinterested the philanthropy, of the gentlemen who have originated this scheme, I do not hesitate, here in my place, upon the solemn responsibilities of a man and a representative, to contend that, in my opinion, it violates that written constitution which we have sworn to support ; that it is pregnant with mischief to the peace and harmony, and, in the estimation of many wise men, with the ultimate destruction of this Union.

"Mr. Chairman, I do not propose to declaim about this, but to discuss it. I scorn to indulge in crimination and recrimination ; and exciting as this topic is, I still indulge the belief that there is good sense enough left—that there is patriotism enough left in this house, to enable us 'to reason together' about it, and to remember that this is not a noisy debating society, gotten up for amusement, but the House of Representatives of a great and proud republic. Sir, I distinctly take the position *that slaves are recognized as property under our constitution ; that in that constitution safeguards to protect this peculiar property are expressly contained ; and that without the incorporation of these safeguards this glorious Union could not have been consummated.* This Federal Government exists under the constitution ; it derives all its power *from* the constitution ; it must be administered by rules prescribed solely *by* that constitution, and possesses no powers but those 'expressly delegated to it.' And I contend, sir, that any act of Congress which prohibits the citizens of the southern states from carrying their slave property with them into territory the common property of the United States, *violates most palpably the faith and compromises of the constitution* ; is unwarranted by any clause contained in that instrument; is sectional, unequal, oppressive; because, while it announces to the citizens of *one* section of the Union that they may go and enjoy this territory with all their property, in the same breath it notifies the citizens of another section, if they go and settle there, they must leave their slave property behind them, in which property they have invested millions of money under the sacred guarantees of the constitution.

"Gentlemen say that the South is dwarfed; that her energies are depressed, her moral character injured, and the days of her glory past. Well, the South, the slaveholding South, gave you WASHINGTON, 'the father of his country'—'first in war, first in peace, and first in the hearts of his countrymen.' The South gave you JEFFERSON, the author of the Declaration of Independence, from which the gentleman from Ohio quoted. Did Mr. Jefferson suppose, when he said that 'all men are created equal,' that this would ever be tortured to support the doctrine that slaves should not be held, when it is known that Mr. Jefferson, who wrote this instrument, was a slaveholder himself all his life, and died a slaveholder? And Mr. MADISON, 'the father of the constitution,' was a slaveholder.

"But gentlemen say we are degenerate. In what, sir, are we so degenerate? In morals?—in patriotism?—in enterprise? No, sir, no. If in olden times we gave you a Washington—the man who carried us through the Revolutionary war—have we not, in later days, given you a Jackson, who led our forces with equal valor and success in the last war? And yet gentlemen say that we are fallen, and that our prosperity is gone! Sir, there is a measure that has oppressed us—the tariff law—which has compelled us to bear heavy burdens for the benefit of the northern and eastern sections of the country. I appeal to the gentlemen of the Northwest, who have stood shoulder to shoulder with the South in the battle of free trade. That victory is consummated, and the farmer of the West, as well as the planter of the South, are now rejoicing under its operation, and basking in its sunshine. I know the patriotism of the Northwest. She has not been appealed to in vain in the cause of commercial freedom, and now she will again favorably respond in the cause of constitutional right. I appeal to the young State of Iowa, which has just come into the Union;—let not her first act be a stab at the constitution. And I know I shall not appeal in vain. I appeal to the patriotism of all. I appeal to the North to remember the spirit which animated their ancestors, and their feeling of devotion to the principles of justice and the Union, which we seek to carry out now. I appeal to the patriotism of this house. Now, when our constellation of liberty is shedding its bright effulgence throughout the world, let it not be dimmed by dividing the cluster. If it be possible let the Federal Union be preserved. Let sectional prejudices be banished from this hall. Let us embark in a generous rivalry to do most in compromising, and compromising forever, and settling forever, this peace-disturbing, this Union-endangering question. But, sir, on *this question the South will maintain her rights—let that be understood*—and these insidious attempts to crush them will be rebuked."

Having served the term for which he was elected, Mr. Dobbin returned home, announced that he was not a candidate for re-election, and again betook himself to his profession. His efforts in Congress gave very general satisfaction to his party, and on his return to the bar, his practice was increased rather than diminished.

Mr. Dobbin has devoted some portion of his leisure to literary pursuits. In 1836 he delivered an address before the Fayetteville Lyceum, which is replete with bright gems and lofty sentiments, and was noticed by E. J. Hale, Esq., in his ably conducted paper, *The Fayetteville Observer*, in the following complimentary terms:

"To say that we were pleased with the lecture delivered by James C. Dobbin, before the Fayetteville Lyceum, would but feebly express our own and the feelings of the large audience who attended on that occasion. To a style flowing, easy and graceful, he united an originality and brilliancy of thought, and enunciation clear and distinct, remarkable for one so young, and giving promise of a future bright fame in the path of his profession, and in that of literature, whose sweets he portrayed in such eloquent language."

We have frequently heard Mr. Dobbin express a high appreciation of this beautifully expressed compliment, as one which he recurs to even now with sincere but melancholy pleasure, as it was the only public compliment that his father lived to hear paid him, and one which he had reason to know his father appreciated highly during the brief remainder of a life then near its close.

In 1840 he delivered an address before the Franklin Library Society, which added to his reputation as an elegant writer and finished orator. On the death of James K. Polk, at the request of the citizens of Fayetteville, he delivered his eulogy.

In June, 1850, he was selected to deliver the annual address before the two literary societies of the University of North Carolina, at Chapel Hill. This address was published at the request of the Philanthropic Society, of which he was a member, and is evidently the emanation of a mind deeply imbued with the bright and beautiful as spread out in nature itself, and as transcribed and reflected in the glowing pages of the great masters of literature.

The allusion to the lamented Judge Gaston, and the address which he delivered at the time Mr. Dobbin graduated, is ingeniously done, and forms the introduction to his own address, and gives him an opportunity of bearing testimony to the truth of Mr. Gaston's teaching, in the following beautiful language:

"Not many years ago it was my lot to form one of the restless throng of college youth, who, with buoyant hopes and eager expectation, sat as anxious listeners, and drank in with general confidence and affectionate admiration, those moral lessons, those encouraging maxims, those warning admonitions, so eloquently, so impressively addressed to us, by the great, the good, and the lamented GASTON. Well do I remember that look of earnest and heartfelt sincerity, with which that venerable man sought to teach us, that 'happiness as well as greatness, enjoyment as well as renown, have no friends so sure as integrity, diligence, and independence;' that 'we are not placed here to waste our days in wanton riot or inglorious ease, with appetites perpetually gratified and never palled, exempted from all care and solicitude, with life ever fresh and joys ever new.' Well do I remember (and may none of us ever forget) that thrilling, heart-moving burst of patriotic eloquence with which he held up to our gaze the gloomy picture of a Union dissolved—the sundered, bleeding limbs of a once gigantic body, instinct with life and health and vigor; his proud exultation that 'still we are great, glorious, united and free;' his touching appeal to the youth then before him, that surely 'such a country and such a constitution have claims which cannot be disregarded.' That eloquent lesson is now familiar to you all, and a student would blush not to know it by heart. That beloved statesman is now beneath the sod. His state mourns his loss, and his memory will ever be cherished by all who appreciate virtue, love excellence, and admire learning. *He* spoke the experience of one who had nearly completed the journey of life, and had himself played no humble part in the race of honorable ambition.

"He who *now* comes at your bidding, hath made but little way in his pilgrimage, and might well be content to return, from the dust and bustle and turmoil of a thus far busy life, for the first time, to his Alma Mater—this starting point in the journey—and assure you who have kindly invited him, and who are now panting to enter on "life's fitful course," that thus far he hath found the maxims of that lamented statesman to be founded in true wisdom—that 'Integrity' *is* the crowning virtue—that 'Labor is not more the duty than the blessing of man'—that our beloved country *does* present to 'the eyes, the hopes, and gratitude of man, a picture as lovely and brilliant,' as he painted it in his loftiest declamation. And well might I now add, that country now—more that ever *now*—challenges all your wisdom, all your virtue, all your patriotism, to uphold and maintain it; to save it from the angry strifes of the *impetuous* and the rash—the mischievous machinations of the *ambitious* and the *selfish*—the reckless madness of misguided *fanaticism*."

He then proceeds to discuss the "exalted pleasures of cultivated taste, and the exquisite enjoyments" of him who can luxuriate in the green pastures, and amid the fragrant flowers of elegant literature." In the midst of his address he makes the following beautiful allusion to President Polk:

"Time was when a stripling youth was seen here on this same hill, struggling with his compeers for the modest prize of the college honors. Stern morality tempered his ambition; diligence bore him through in triumph; parental smiles and greeting friends cheered him as he was decked with the university honors. Time passed on. A vast multitude throng the eastern portico of the capitol of the republic. Fashion and wealth, the curious and the gay, the great men and wise of the land are there. For a moment solemn stillness pervades that assembly; then the air is rent with the shouts of rejoicing; for a great people have just placed upon the brows of a statesman the highest honors of the proudest republic on earth! Let the aspiring student learn and be encouraged by the interesting truth, that *that statesman* was the stripling boy, who began by winning his first honors at the University of North Carolina, and ended by wearing that of a mighty republic."

He next proceeds to address the graduating class, and endeavors to impress upon their minds love of country, and a true appreciation of the inestimable value of the Union, in the following language:

"And what a country too is that in which your lot is cast, that makes us *all* glory in the name of American citizens—that makes us all so proud of the past, so proud of the present, so hopeful of the 'shadowy future!' Poetic imagination is overtasked in the effort to picture its real grandeur; so changeful the scene, so rapid the transition, so wonderful its strides from infant weakness to giant manhood! *Once* a mighty wilderness, a continent of unquelled forests, the home of the fierce savage and the howling panther; *now* a beautiful land of cultivated fields, and filled with statesmen, orators, and philosophers! Once a modest flag, adorned with thirteen stars, affixed to a flagstaff planted between the mountains and the Atlantic, waved over three millions of American freemen; *now* a broad ensign, bearing on its ample folds, not *thirteen*, but *thirty* stars, nailed to a flagstaff, planted, not on the narrow confines between the mountains and the Atlantic, but *on* the mountains, on the valleys of the Atlantic and the Pacific, and the great gulf of the south—affording protection not to three but to twenty millions of free citizens of an "ocean-bound republic!" Of other lands poetic prophecy reveals only sad visions of decay and downfall. British genius hath already written of our father land—

"'England, like Greece, shall fall despoiled, defaced,
And weep, the Tadmor of the watery waste.
The wave shall mock her lone and manless shore,
The deep shall know her freighted wealth no more;
And unborn wanderers in the future wood,
Where London stands, shall ask where London stood.'

"But if American sons prove worthy of American sires;—if education be truly the protectress of liberty;—if time and Christianity, instead of elevating and blessing, have not debased man—*yours* is the land whose future grandeur and magnificence will continue to baffle the conceptions of the wildest imagination. We read in sacred history, that for the preservation of the human family, Noah was seen constructing an ark. The fancy of the gifted Headley has graphically painted the scene,—that as the huge edifice went up, 'The farmer returned at evening from his field, and the gay citizen of the town drove past and christened it 'Noah's Folly,' and the workmen upon it laughed as they drove the nails and hewed the plank. But when the terrible storm came—upborne on the flood, the heaven-protected ark rose above the buried cities and mountains, and floated away on the shoreless deep. And when the deluge was stayed, with its inmates unharmed, it at last safely reposed on the summit of the sacred mountain Ararat.' We read too in profane history that time was when our Washington was seen constructing a political, a republican ark, for the final protection of human liberty. When with his sage compeers he was rearing the novel edifice, and constructing it of rafters and beams of republican simplicity and popular freedom, titled nobility and ribboned pride in other lands mocked and smiled at it as *unfit* for the storms that would surely assail it. But this far, under the blessings of Providence, amid the terrible events that ever and anon have crushed the rights of man elsewhere—amid angry storms and the wildest billows of party rage—upborne on the flood, *our* heaven-protected ark of freedom *still* floats on, and amid the tempests at their darkest hour there has *still* continued to stream from it a steady light to cheer and gladden and encourage. And when that most terrific of tempests shall come—(which may God in his mercy avert!)—when domestic fanaticism or party rage shall triumph—when the voice of patriotism shall for a moment be hushed amid the hoarse clamor of discordant factions—when the flood of fraternal strife and sectional hostility shall for a moment deluge the land—*still* may we not cling to the hope of the father of his country, that when it shall please heaven to stay the storm, our ark may also find *its* sacred resting-place, *and that may be on the glorious Union of the States.*"

In the summer of 1848, Mr. Dobbin was importuned to become a candidate for the House of Commons, in the Legislature of North Carolina. He was elected, and on his first appearance in the house was put in nomination as the democratic candidate for speaker, in opposition to that sterling whig, Robert B. Gilliam, Esq., of Granville county. For three days the balloting was continued without an election, so nearly was the house divided. On the fourth day, Mr. Dobbin authorized his friend Daniel W. Courto, Esq., of Rockingham, to withdraw his name from before the body, whereupon Mr. Gilliam was elected, and the house soon after organized. Mr. Dobbin was placed upon the judiciary committee and took a prominent part in all its deliberations, as well as a distinguished part in the discussion of all the important matters before the house. At this session of the legislature, the philanthropist Miss Dix memorialized that body to erect an asylum for the insane. The memorial was referred to a select committee, of which John W. Ellis, Esq., of Rowan, was chairman, and through him a bill was reported to the house, favorable to the prayer of the memorialist. In the mean time Mr. Ellis was elected one of the judges of the Superior Court, and forthwith resigned his seat in the legislature. Some days after, the Hon. Kenneth Rayner moved that the bill introduced by Mr. Ellis on the subject of the asylum, be taken up, and that one hundred thousand dollars be appropriated for its erection. This motion Mr. Rayner seconded in a speech of great power, eloquence and beauty; but the motion was negatived by a vote, ayes 44, noes 66, under circumstances which induced the belief the bill could not pass. The amiable and beloved wife of Mr. Dobbin, a day or two before Mr. Rayner spoke, had just been committed to her mother earth, and he was not in attendance on the house. Miss Dix, anxious for the fate of the bill, and having confidence in Mr. Dobbin's influence and power before the legislature, had him waited upon, and *reminded of his wife's request that he would advocate and support that measure.* The appeal could not be withstood and he promised to *try* on the coming day.

When the house met, Mr. Dobbin was present. The bill had been reconsidered on the previous day, and was pending on a motion to appropriate $25,000. This amount Mr. Dobbin moved to strike out, and proposed as a substitute a plan to impose a tax that in four years would raise the sum of $85,000; and in the advocacy of the measure he delivered one of the most eloquent, thrilling and heart-touching speeches that was ever delivered in the capitol of North Carolina. On resuming his seat, the bill passed its second reading by a vote of 101 ayes to 10 noes. The rules were immediately suspended, on motion of the Hon. Edward Stanley, that the bill might be put upon its third reading, which it passed by a vote of 91 to 9, and nearly every one of the *nine* assigned some special reason why he had not voted in the affirmative. The *Raleigh Register*, a whig paper, in alluding to Mr. Dobbin's speech upon the asylum bill, says: "The speech of Mr. Dobbin, in favor of the bill, was one of the most touchingly beautiful efforts that we have ever heard. Its noble and eloquent conception, impressive delivery, and the circumstances which prompted and attended it, all combined to render it truly worthy the occasion."

Another leading whig paper, the *Fayetteville Observer*, says, "There were few dry eyes in the large assembly of members and audience during Mr. Dobbin's speech."

At the same session of the legislature, the Central Rail-road bill was introduced, which proposed that North Carolina should subscribe two million dollars towards completing the scheme. The fate of the bill was for a long time doubtful. The route proposed was not calculated directly to benefit Mr. Dobbin's county, and many contended the road would materially injure his constituents. Mr. Dobbin listened for a while to all that could be said for and against the measure — discarded strictly sectional legislation as detrimental even to the interests of those counties that apparently received no benefit, and finally gave vent to his liberal and patriotic sentiments in a speech of great power and beauty, in which he declared that the glory, the honor, and prosperity of his native state, were matters of far higher importance in his estimation, than any political distinction that could await him, and whatever the result might be upon his destiny, he was prepared to abide it, rather than that his beloved state—a pattern to others for the practice of honesty and integrity, and all the comely virtues which the nation felt proud of, should be pointed at as a state that slept whilst her younger sisters labored — a state that retrograded whilst others prospered and became a lure to tempt our children to forsake the homesteads of their fathers and the state of their nativity. The bill passed, and the *Register*, in alluding to Mr. Dobbin's effort in its behalf, says, "Mr. Dobbin was frequently applauded by the members in spite of the chairman's efforts to preserve decorum. Indeed, a man must be stoically indifferent to the welfare of his state, not to be moved by such eloquent appeals."

The influence of Mr. Dobbin in the legislature was strongly exemplified in the fate of a bill which he superintended in the house for the benefit of his immediate constituents. It was a bill for the erection of a plank road from Fayetteville to Salisbury. It was the *first plank road projected in North Carolina*, or indeed in any southern state ; and when Mr. Dobbin asked for an appropriation of $80,000 from the state to aid in its completion, the *members smiled*, and voted the proposition down. On a future day he had the bill reconsidered, and substituted $120,000 for $80,000, and after elucidating the subject, and contending that it would be a profitable investment on the part of the state, the bill passed ; and every assertion made by Mr. Dobbin has been more than realized, the state having made a net profit thus far of $2,647 37, from the fact that the dividends and premiums on the state bonds have exceeded the amount of interest paid on the investment. The result now is, that plank roads are looked upon with universal favor throughout North Carolina, and in all the other southern states. At this session of the legislature we believe Mr. Dobbin could have attained a seat upon the Superior Court bench, in supply of one of the two vacancies that existed, but it is understood he declined being put in nomination, preferring to practise at the bar, rather than to preside on the bench, the more especially as his practice yields a much larger revenue than the salary of a judge. Mr. Dobbin was returned to the next session of the legislature, and on the first ballot was elected speaker of the House of Commons. The debates were strong and violent, but the impartial, mild and dignified bearing of the speaker commanded respect, and his call to order, in a voice peculiarly clear and distinct, invariably had the desired effect.

As a legal adviser Mr. Dobbin is remarkably cautious in coming to conclusions, is a sound lawyer and safe counsellor. He seldom gives an off-hand opinion, and generally consults authorities before he ventures to advise. But this once done, he is firm in his position, and invariably sustains himself with an ability that generally commands success. In North Carolina we have more learned jurists than James C. Dobbin, but in the combined character of lawyer and advocate he has few superiors in the state. In the management of his causes before a jury, he excels in an eminent degree. Sometimes he addresses them in a plain, simple, colloquial strain, which is best described under the appellation of a *free* and *easy chat*, during which a perfect understanding between him and the jury seems to be established. This done, he rises as the occasion demands, and leads his hearers from point to point with a directness and clearness that leaves them no room to mistake his aim. If the cause demands a lengthy argument it is interspersed with episodes of a pleasant and agreeable character, that rarely fail to interest and please. The character of Mr. Dobbin's eloquence is somewhat difficult to describe. It is always calm, mild, insinuating and persuasive, resembling usually the gentle rivulet more than the mountain torrent, until some passing incident suggests a bright thought or beautiful figure ; suddenly the scene is changed, the inspiration of the moment lends a new charm to all he says—the bright conceptions of his mind are clothed in drapery the most chaste and beautiful, and whilst his clear but mellow voice discourses music to the ear, the susceptibilities of his own nature are roused into lively action, and find a ready sympathy in the tender feelings of the heart.

By this rare combination of gifts he is enabled to please, win, captivate and affect the heart, and convince the judgment, and is almost irresistible before a jury when the issue is life or death. Another element of Mr. Dobbin's success may be traced to his skill in the examination of a witness, whether he is for or against his client, and the peculiar *tact* which he possesses in the management of the most minute circumstance that may exist in his cause. We may be mistaken in our attempt to disclose the elements of Mr. Dobbin's success. Be that as it may, the fact is indisputable, no man of his age in North Carolina has been so successful in the management of capital criminal causes. It is now a rare thing for a felon to be tried on his circuit, but that he is employed for the defence. We have heard him prosecute, and have listened to his efforts, even then with delight, but have always thought that he labored as if under some restraint, and have fancied that the difference between his defence and prosecution was as the difference between the song of a sweet warbler in the free and open air, and the same bird attempting to sing when imprisoned within a fowler's cage. We cannot better give an estimate of Mr. Dobbin's eloquence, in his moments of happy inspiration, than by a reference to the part he bore in the late national democratic convention in Baltimore. Forty-eight ballots had been cast, and apparently the nomination of a candidate for President was as far distant as ever, and the wildest excitement prevailed throughout the vast assemblage. For *ten successive ballotings* the name of Franklin Pierce had fallen still-born upon the convention, as Virginia on the 37th, and Maine and New-Hampshire and Virginia on the 38th ballot, and so on to the 48th inclusive, had voted for Mr. Pierce. Still no enthusiasm was yet created in his behalf, and no other states seemed ready to wheel into line. On the 49th ballot, North Carolina had determined to cast her vote for Franklin Pierce, and James C. Dobbin was about to give it. It was not in his nature, at such a time, to cast a *silent vote*. He felt that the wild and conflicting elements needed but a master-mind to grasp and wield them to a new candidate. He made the attempt, and in a burst of eloquence swept the convention to the flood, which led to Pierce's nomination. Even the Virginia papers award to Mr. Dobbin the high credit we have just assigned to him. The *Norfolk Argus* says, "The effect of Mr. Dobbin's speech was magical. Georgia followed North Carolina, then came Alabama, and then state after state in rapid succession, until 283 votes were recorded for the brave son of the granite state, and in the twinkling of an eye all was sunshine and enthusiasm, where but an instant before clouds had cast their shadows." And a correspondent of the same paper says: "You are right in according to the Hon. J. C. Dobbin, of Fayetteville, N. C., the honor of creating the 'magical effect' which carried the nomination of General Pierce as with a whirlwind." And the *Southside Democrat*, published in Petersburgh, satisfied that Virginia had the honor of first voting for Mr. Pierce, says, "It was the Hon. James C. Dobbin, of Fayetteville, N. C., who announced the vote of North Carolina, and at the same time spoke in favor of Gen. Pierce's nomination. This speech of Mr. Dobbin was decidedly the best speech made in the convention. It was made at a critical moment, it was exactly to the purpose, it was eloquent and stirring. In our opinion *it contributed more to the nomination of Gen*

Pierce than all other causes combined. It excited an enthusiasm for him which spread like fire throughout the southern delegation."

In the private walks of life Mr. Dobbin is beloved and held in high estimation by all who know him, and possesses the confidence and affections of a large number of friends and admirers. In his habits he is somewhat retired, and seems to prefer the family circle, and its joys and pleasures, more than the amusements of fashionable life. Mr. Dobbin, in 1838, married Louisa, daughter of the late Gabriel Holmes, of New-Hanover. He has for a number of years been a consistent member of the Presbyterian church. He is yet a young man, but one on whom the hopes of many in North Carolina are centred, as one who will adorn any station—as one who, if spared, will add lustre to the *virtues* which already characterize and distinguish the Old North State.

NOTE.—Since this sketch was written, Mr. D. has served another session in the legislature, and been appointed Secretary of the Navy; of the impression made by his appointment, and the reception it has met from the press and people, we need say nothing. Men of all parties endorse the sagacity of the President in the selection he has made.—J. L.

Eng'd by H.B. Hall.

Jeffn. Davis

SECRETARY OF WAR.

Eng'd for Biographical Sketches of Eminent Americans.

JEFFERSON DAVIS,

SECRETARY OF WAR.

COLONEL JEFFERSON DAVIS, the subject of this memoir, is a native of Kentucky. During infancy, his father removed to the Territory of Mississippi, now Wilkinson county. Young Davis, after an academic course at home, entered Transylvania College, Kentucky, where he remained until his appointment as cadet, and was sent to the United States Military Academy at West Point in 1842.

In June, 1828, he graduated at that institution, was appointed a brevet second Lieutenant, and served as an infantry and staff officer upon the Northern frontier until 1833, exhibiting such ability that he was then promoted to a first lieutenancy in the new regiment of Dragoons. He served throughout the celebrated "Black Hawk war" in the North West, doing efficient service, often being detailed upon important and dangerous duties. During this campaign, the celebrated Indian chief, Black Hawk, was captured, and while in captivity he formed an attachment for the gallant young Lieutenant that only ceased with the life of that brave Indian. From 1833 to 1835 he served on the Western frontier, and was engaged in the expedition against the Camanches and Pawnees, which first penetrated their mountain fastnesses, and reduced them to the necessity of sueing for a treaty of peace.

In 1835 he resigned his commission, and returned to Mississippi, resuming civil life in the peaceful occupation of a cotton planter,—employing his leisure hours in the prosecution of those studies, a thorough knowledge of which has since enabled him to take an enviable stand among the statesmen and practically scientific men of the day. Thus engaged,

"*Far from the madding crowd's ignoble strife,*"

he remained but little known beyond his immediate neighborhood, until 1843, when he emerged into public life, taking an active part in behalf of the democracy of his state, making such an impression upon the people, that in 1844 they chose him Presidential elector for the state at large, on the "Polk and Dallas" ticket. In November, 1845, he was elected congressional representative, in which capacity he remained until July, 1846, when, although absent from his state attending Congress, he was unanimously elected their Colonel by the celebrated first regiment of Mississippi volunteers, then enlisting for the war with Mexico. Upon notification of this, he immediately resigned his seat in Congress, and after procuring for his regiment, against much opposition and prejudice, the arms since so celebrated, and known from the effective use his men made of them, as the "Mississippi Rifles," he hastened to join his men at New Orleans, *en route* for the seat of war, and soon reinforced General Taylor upon the Rio Grande.

It would far exceed the limits of this memoir to give even a *resumé* of the part which he, with his gallant Mississippians, took in that memorable campaign. Suffice it to say that he won for himself a memorable name at Monterey and Buena Vista,—the part that he took in the latter victory being such that he is now familiarly known by the *sobriquet* of "Buena Vista."

The late General Taylor, in his dispatch of March 6th, 1847, with characteristic brevity, says: "The Mississippi riflemen, under Col. Davis, were highly conspicuous for their gallantry and steadiness, and sustained throughout the engagement the reputation of veteran troops. Brought into action against an immensely superior force, they maintained themselves for a long time unsupported, and with heavy loss, and held an important part in the field until reinforced. *Col. Davis, though severely wounded, remained in the saddle until the close of the action. His distinguished coolness and gallantry at the head of his regiment on this day entitle him to the particular notice of the government.*"

At the expiration of the term of enlistment of his regiment, he was ordered home with the mere handful that was left of his gallant men; and while in New Orleans, he received from President Polk a commission as Brigadier General of volunteers. Considering this an invasion of the rights of the States—a power usurped by Congress and by them vested in the President—and a violation of that provision of the Constitution which reserves to the States respectively the appointment of the officers of the militia, he consistently declined the tempting offer, and continued his homeward journey by the Mississippi river to enjoy domestic quiet, and recover of a wound received at Buena Vista which threatened to maim him for life.

His progress homeward was a continuous triumphal procession.

In 1847 he received an Executive appointment as United States Senator to fill a vacancy, and at the ensuing session of the State Legislature, was *unanimously* elected to the same post for the next six years.

The following incident, which is said to have occurred while he was a member of the House, will serve to illustrate the high promise of statesmanship exhibited by him in his first speech before that body.

It was the habit of ex-President John Q. Adams, then in the House of Representatives, to closely observe new members, always seating himself near when they were about making their Parliamentary *debut*, eyeing them and listening attentively—sitting out their speech if it pleased him, but soon leaving if it did not. When Colonel Davis had arisen for the first time on the floor, Mr. Adams, as usual, took a seat near him, and was soon absorbed in close attention. Those who knew this habit of the "old man eloquent," soon perceived that the new member had impressed him deeply. He sat until the conclusion of the speech —his attention riveted upon the orator; and then arose, and crossing over to some of his friends, remarked, "That young man, gentlemen, is no ordinary man. He will make his mark yet, mind me."

While in the Senate, he was chairman of the committee on military affairs, rendering, by reason of his thorough acquaintance with its business, efficient service to that branch of the government he now administers so ably. Being a Southerner, a Jeffersonian State's Rights man, and a believer in the "right of instruction," he took an active part in the debates of the day upon the slavery questions, advocating the rights of the STATES and of the South so ably as at once to place himself in the front rank of the Democratic leaders.

In September, 1851, after the withdrawal of General Quitman as candidate for Governor of Mississippi, Colonel Davis accepted a call of the democracy to fill the vacant candidacy, and at once resigned his seat in the Senate from a principle entertained by him that the public had a right to indicate his post of duty, and that no citizen should be a candidate for one office while holding another. Although he became a candidate only some four or five weeks before the election took place, and was suffering from severe illness during that time, while his opponent had been stumping the State for several months before the Colonel's announcement of his acceptance, and continued to do so zealously to the last day of the canvass: still, by the popularity of his name alone, Mr. Davis reduced the majority that the opposition had shown at the "Convention election," two months previous, of some 7,500 to only 999. Had the election been but a week or two later, or had he been able to take the stump, it is both demonstrated by the figures, and admitted by his opponents, that he would have triumphed.

He remained upon his plantation, Briarfield, content in the quiet of his family, only leaving home to advocate, in his own State, Louisiana, and Tennessee, the election of General Pierce, until his appointment as Secretary of War, the post he now holds with so much credit to the choice of the President, and advantage to that arm of the Government.

In stature, Colonel Davis is of medium size, slender and straight: his habits active, energetic, and assiduous; his carriage dignified and military. His manners are affable, courteous, and frank; his passions—slow to work—are deep and lasting, his friendships and enmities being equally hearty. His mind is active; his judgment strong; his perceptions clear; his reflection deep, and his acquirements thorough and extensive.

In politics, he is a Jeffersonian and a strict constructionist. As a public man, he has ever acted upon his cardinal principle, that no one should seek office; or, having become a public man, decline to serve the people in whatever capacity they should desire his services; that having become a public man, he is, so long as he remains such, a *servant* of the people, and, as such, should permit them, rather than himself, to choose in what capacity he should act.

A stranger would at once say of Mr. Davis, that he was a clear, strong-headed, common-sense man; cautious and wary in taking his premises, certain and irresistible in his conclusions from them. This is the secret of his success in life—*he never commits a folly.* It is to his practical sagacity, in a great measure, that he is indebted for his success. No art of his adversary can draw him into collateral or immaterial issues; he selects the best ground, and wages his battle *there.* Although his acquaintance with books is large, yet he makes no unnecessary display of learning. As a speaker, Mr. Davis is earnest and fluent—his language, though never ornate, is always vigorous; and it may safely be said that he never uses two words where one will answer his purpose.

We should be glad to add to our notice of him as a public man, from the materials at hand, a few of those incidents which reveal so accurately the personal traits of his character; but the design of our work will limit us. As a private citizen, he is no less entitled to praise than as a faithful public officer; it is the perfect private citizen who makes the perfect public man.

His success in life has been the result of his own exertions, and not of that good luck which the world (little understanding what the word imports) so often ascribes to those who rise unaided to distinction. No man knew better how to time his efforts; and while he never wasted his force on worthless and unattainable objects, he well knew when to take advantage of opportunities—and when once he decided, no man pursued his object with more fearlessness or energy. Free from all intolerance of spirit, he yet never fails to show his scorn of falsehood or meanness. Without ostentation, either in his manners or style of life, he always maintains the air and polish of a gentleman, and lives surrounded by all the elegance and refinements which are the type of a well disciplined taste.

We commend his example to the young men of our country who yearn for honor and reward. There is a noble field in our great Republic, where our institutions not only guarantee the freest competition, but invite it.

Eng^d by F. Halpin.

ATTORNEY GENERAL FOR THE UNITED STATES.

Engraved for Biographical Sketches of Eminent

CALEB CUSHING,

ATTORNEY GENERAL OF THE UNITED STATES,

Is well known throughout the United States as a distinguished politician and eminent scholar. Mr. Cushing was born in Salisbury, Essex County, Massachusetts, in January, 1800, and consequently is now in his fifty-fourth year. His father, belonging to one of the most respectable old families of Massachusetts, was extensively engaged in the shipping business, by which he acquired a handsome fortune. Caleb Cushing entered Harvard College when very young, and graduated in the eighteenth year of his age. He commenced the study of the law at Cambridge, and was appointed tutor of mathematics and natural philosophy in Harvard College, which place he held for two years, and then removed to Newburyport, to engage in the practice of law. In his profession he was very successful, and acquired the reputation of a good lawyer. The political career of Mr. Cushing commenced in 1825, when he was chosen a representative from Newburyport to the lower house of the Massachusetts Legislature. In 1826, he was elected a member of the State Senate. Both these places he filled with ability, and to the satisfaction of his constituents. After this he continued in the practice of the law for two years; and in 1829 he went to Europe on a tour of pleasure and observation. On his return, he prepared for the press and published his "Reminiscences of Spain," a work which added much to his literary reputation. He also appeared as the author of a "Historical and Political Review of the Revolution in France," in 1830. About the same time he was a contributor to the North American Review, writing mainly on historical and legal subjects. Mr. Cushing was again elected to the Massachusetts Legislature in 1833 and 1834. He made several unsuccessful runs for Congress, but was finally elected to represent the North Essex District in 1835. His congressional career continued for four consecutive terms, or eight years, viz: from 1835 to 1843. Having commenced public life as a friend of John Quincy Adams, Mr. Cushing acted with the whig party, both in the State Legislature and in Congress, until the administration of John Tyler, when he was one of the few whigs who ventured to sustain the course of that president in abandoning his political friends. The consequence to Mr. Cushing was his separation from the whig party, and eventually his connexion with the democratic party for the last ten years.

As a member of Congress he evinced decided ability, and his speeches and reports showed in the most favorable light his statesmanlike qualification. In 1843, President Tyler nominated Mr. Cushing as one of his cabinet, but the Senate refused to confirm the nomination, owing to his political course and the peculiar position of parties at the time. Thereupon the president nominated him as commissioner to China, and the Senate assented to the appointment. He left the United States in the summer of 1843, and proceeded to China by the Mediterranean and overland route. In 1844, he negotiated a treaty with the Chinese government, establishing, for the first time, diplomatic relations between the two countries. He returned to the United States by way of Mexico, having accomplished the important business of his mission, and passed around the globe within the short period of a year. On his return home, Mr. Cushing made a visit to Minnesota Territory, as was supposed for the purpose of taking up his residence there. He, however, returned to Newburyport in 1846, and was again elected to represent that town in the legislature. In that body he was the most prominent member at the session of 1847, when the Mexican war was at its height. He acted with the democratic members in advocating the policy of that war, and for appropriating $20,000 for equipping the Massachusetts Regiment of Volunteers, at the expense of the State. When this proposition was defeated, Mr. Cushing advanced the money from his own means, and the regiment was made ready for service.

He was chosen colonel of the regiment, and accompanied it to the Rio Grande, in Mexico, in the spring of 1847, being attached to the army under command of General Taylor. Soon after his arrival in the Mexican territory, he was appointed a Brigadier General in the United States army, and several regiments of volunteers were placed under his command. Hostilities having ceased on the northern line, General Cushing being anxious for more active service, was, at his own request, transferred to the army of General Scott. It was not, however, his fortune to be engaged in any of the brilliant actions of the war; and after various services as a commandant at San Angel and other places, he returned home on the restoration of peace. In 1847, while he was in Mexico, General Cushing was nominated by the democrats of Massachusetts as their candidate for governor. This movement was owing to the part he had taken in support of the war, and was done without consultation with him. It doubtless greatly improved his position with the democratic party in the State and nation, and the increased, though of course, unsuccessful vote given to him, compared with the democratic vote of the previous year, was flattering to General Cushing, and his friends who had urged the nomination. In 1848, General Cushing was a zealous laborer in behalf of the election of General Cass, acting on all occasions with the union democrats and against the free soil party. In 1850, he was, for the fifth time, elected a member of the legislature from Newburyport, and was active in that body in opposing the coalition of the democrats with the free soil party, which caused the election of Charles Sumner to the United States Senate. In 1851, the office of Attorney General of Massachusetts was offered to General Cushing by Governor Boutwell, but he declined the honor. The legislature of 1852 having created an additional Justice of the Supreme Court, General Cushing was appointed to the office. It is admitted that he performed the duties of his seat on the bench with ability and integrity, and as a judge, he acquired an enviable popularity. In person, General Cushing is tall and slender, with dark complexion and pleasing address. His habits are of the most active and industrious character, and his friends have great confidence that he will acquit himself in the duties of a cabinet office with the same ability that he has shown in the various other public stations he has occupied.

There are some men so nicely tempered in the elements of their being that, to use the language of natural science, they seem formed to be "perfect conductors" of the better sympathies, at least, of all with whom they are thrown into contact. Without any conscious effort or design on their part, and, indeed, because they cannot avoid it, they enter at once into the feelings and appreciate the views of others around them, and find their hearts beating in unison with the circle of which they happen, for the time, to form a part. They are instinctively interested in others, and have the power of interesting others in themselves without any conscious effort to do so. A free interchange of thought and feeling between themselves and others takes place almost at the moment of contact, and they have the happy art of throwing themselves at once into the position of other minds, and of appreciating such views of things as that position presents. To pronounce such men insincere, unstable, and destitute of any fixed opinions and principles—to regard them as under the control of mere selfish policy and aiming at universal popular favor, would evince an utter want of discrimination, and would be the grossest misrepresentation of the class of men whom we are describing.

Receiving from the hands of his Maker a temperament of this peculiar character, General Cushing is happily fitted for distinction both in social and professional life, and for the general offices of a public speaker; and to this temperament in part, must be attributed his achieved and acknowledged eminence in each of these particulars. It would not be easy for him to avoid being the life of every social circle of which he is a part, or becoming thoroughly identified for the time with his client, or engaging the attention at once of any assembly in which he is called to speak. With a ready command of language, for which he is indebted in part to the habitual reading of the best writers of our own tongue, and of the classics of other languages, and a happy susceptibility by which he kindles at once with the spirit of his occasion, he is never long on his feet without saying what the occasion demands, and making himself understood and felt.

As to the peculiar cast of General Cushing's mind as it developes itself, especially in his forensic efforts, it is rather to be classed with such as seize at once upon the great and broad principles of justice and common sense in the case, and bring those principles to bear, than among that class which spend their strength in eliminating nice and subtle distinctions, and which astonish others by the precision with which such distinctions are drawn out. Though blessed by a kind Providence with the means of securing a library of extensive range and of great value, the materials which he draws from this resource are never paraded for display, nor can his mind be characterized as a depository of the thoughts of other men; though he still knows how, with singular propriety, when occasion requires, to apply a choice saying, either of the ancients or moderns, to a passing exigency.

General Cushing excels many eminent men in his thorough knowledge of human nature, and in his quick and instinctive insight into the character of individual men. He knows how to approach men of all classes and of all prejudices, and to impress himself upon them; and if there be any weakness especially, either in the character or the argument of his adversary, none is more ready than he to lay his finger upon it, and hold it up in a clear and striking light.

Another characteristic by which General Cushing is happily fitted for the office of an advocate, and of a general public speaker, is a ready facility in illustration, and a command of those materials for this purpose which are supplied by the conduct and sayings of others with whom he has been brought into contact, either by personal acquaintance or by reading. Throwing himself, in his illustrations and anecdotes, as his temperament qualifies him to do, into the position and feelings of those of whom he is speaking, his narrations are always vivid and possessed of a quickening power; and if there be any man who knows how to associate ideas in a manner at once natural and yet unusual and striking, so as to produce a pleasurable surprise and wake up even a sluggish and melancholy mind, it is certainly he.

With no time or disposition to enter into the practical and laborious part of agricultural life, or of horticulture, his tastes run decidedly in that direction, and his means allow him to indulge them. To listen to him in an agricultural meeting, or in a road-side conversation with an agricultural man, one would easily discover that he had much real sympathy with that class of men.

In his theological views and sympathies he is about equally removed from that class of theologians, who look for everything good and true, and important, only in the past, and from those who despise the ancients, and seem to have no regard but for things either new or future; and he would take as much pleasure in discovering and magnifying a point of agreement between himself and a controversialist of another sect, as some men do in holding up and substantiating a point of difference. With his tendencies toward a medium between both extremes of ultraism, he would be equally at home and equally in place in leading onward in some mental movement, or in holding back and moderating a movement as the exigency might require.

The above outline denotes a life of varied action not often to be met with. From a graduate at an early age, we trace him to the tutor, the lawyer, traveller, legislator, diplomatist, explorer, and soldier, and in each successive sphere of employment we find the same perseverance, irrepressible activity, indomitable energy, and capacity to meet the requirements of any branch of the public service.

Without taking into the account his orations and occasional addresses before literary and scientific institutions, his literary, historical, and political productions have been very numerous. Although he stands in the foremost rank as a debater and public speaker, prompt, fluent, vigorous, and self-possessed, his ability in this respect does not form the principal feature in his intellectual character. He possesses an intrepid and executive genius. There is work, resolution, and endurance in him, as well as learning, eloquence, and facility in literary composition.

His energy and vigor, both of mind and body, his thorough acquaintance with all the higher business of life, civil and military; his command of speech and pen, and the adaptability of his talents, and generality of his acquirements, remind us of the men of the same traits of character and the same versatility of life, who figure, under similar circumstances, in the annals of the ancient republics.

Eng'd by H.B. Hall.

James Campbell

UNITED STATES POST MASTER GENERAL

Eng'd for Biographical Sketches of Eminent Americans.

JAMES CAMPBELL,

POSTMASTER-GENERAL.

The present Postmaster-General of the United States, is the youngest member of the cabinet of President Pierce, except the Secretary of the Navy, Mr. Dobbin. Mr. Dobbin is thirty-nine years of age, and Mr. Campbell forty. It is a significant characteristic of American progress that our young men wield great, if not commanding power in public affairs. Nor is this the case to the exclusion of men of riper years. It is the result of a great political and social necessity. Fortunes, in this country, are constantly changing hands, and we have no such institutions fostered by our laws as the system of old and honorable families. The son of the rich man of to-day, may, in his turn, be the father of the poor man of to-morrow. Nor are the glittering heights of fame and influence always attainable by the offspring of wealthy parents. Hence it is, that self-education and self-reliance are the marked elements of the American character. Hence it is, that long before an Englishman may be said to be ready to begin the world, the citizen in this great Republic is probably an influential legislator, or a leading man in his own community. The amount of service that one man may thus confer upon his country and upon his fellow beings, cannot very readily be over-estimated. Our old men are not the less serviceable because they begin public life early. The school they pass through before they reach the Psalmist's age, is not only valuable to them but to their children, and their children's children, and thus the intellects that pass from the stage are constantly revived and renewed in those who follow them.

James Campbell is the son of an adopted citizen. His father emigrated from Ireland, at the close of the last century; and by his industry and thrift, was enabled to give his children a thorough education. The object of our sketch exhibited, at an early day, those sterling traits of character which have made him so influential and so successful through life. He became a member of the bar, resolved upon success. His persevering, energetic, prompt, and inquiring mind soon gave him a high rank among the proverbially able, acute, and eloquent members of the legal profession in Philadelphia; and at the age of twenty-nine he was appointed judge of the court of common pleas of that city and county—having been unanimously recommended for that station by the delegates in the Legislature from the county, and unanimously confirmed by the state senate. His position was well calculated to task his intellect and his firmness; but, during nine years, he discharged its various duties, onerous and exacting, to the satisfaction of all parties. At the end of that time (1850), the Judiciary was made elective, by a change in the constitution of Pennsylvania; and at the first ensuing election, in 1851, Judge Campbell, while on the common pleas bench, was nominated by the democratic party one of the five democratic candidates for the supreme court of the state. The Convention which placed his name before the people for that high position was composed mainly of lawyers, including some of the most eminent and distinguished intellects of the state. Two thirds of this body voted for the nomination of Judge Campbell. In their address to the people, sustaining their selections, they spoke of Judge Campbell in the following eloquent terms:—

"Naturally modest and unobtrusive, although possessed of excellent talents and extensive legal attainments, he has not sought opportunities to exhibit himself before the public. He has performed his duties with exemplary fidelity, and his legal opinions have been marked for their accuracy, perspicuity, and system. In all the relations of life, Judge Campbell has sustained an unblemished reputation. Pure, well educated, honest, and inflexible; combining with these, gentlemanly deportment and manners, he possesses a strong mind and sound judgment. He has a large circle of warm and devoted friends, who have known him from his youth, and who rejoice in his elevation, by the energy of his character, to the position which he holds, and also cherish him for his integrity, talents, and social virtues."

But, notwithstanding this high tribute to a tried and trusted jurist, and to an esteemed and irreproachable citizen, he was defeated at the election. It is not necessary that we should dwell upon the causes which produced this result. Suffice it to say that Judge Campbell was defeated solely by a sectarian combination of bigotry and intolerance. During all this excitement, however—even while pursued and persecuted —he bore himself with a fortitude and calmness which elicited spontaneous admiration. So well established was the character of Judge Campbell, and so wide and general the feeling which followed the result of the election in 1851, that as soon as Mr. Bigler, the popular and intrepid chief magistrate of Pennsylvania, elected that year, came to select his cabinet counsellors, the name of James Campbell was pointed out, by emphatic demonstrations of public opinion, as one that would be most satisfactory to the democratic masses. Governor Bigler accordingly appointed him attorney-general, in January, 1852. That he filled this high trust with eminent ability, sagacity, and energy, even his adversaries have never denied. During the presidential election of 1852, Judge Campbell was enabled to render great and signal service to the democratic party. Owing to circumstances, the state was for a time regarded as extremely doubtful; and it was in that crisis his high and patriotic character shone conspicuous. Nobly forgetting the personal injury inflicted by those of his own party who had caused his defeat, and mindful only of his duty to his principles, he threw himself into the contest, and, with enthusiastic perseverance and ability, devoted himself to the work. Thousands remembered his own defeat in the feelings of deep and resistless indignation; and, to add to their feelings arising from this cause, the whig leaders were energetically attempting to arouse their prejudices against President Pierce himself. Judge Campbell boldly took issue with this movement; and it is not going too far to say that to his appeals, to his eloquence, to his tact and skill, were the democracy indebted for the reconciliation which followed. Indeed, it was then, as it is now, admitted, that to him more than to any other man was Pennsylvania indebted for the two signal victories in October and November, 1852.

When President Pierce called Judge Campbell into his cabinet, he acted upon that knowledge of politics and of men, which is so strongly his characteristic. He knew the history, as well as the tone and temper of the new postmaster-general. Judge Campbell has now been about nine months at the head of that most intricate and responsible department. That he is a popular executive officer, even his opponents admit, and that he is prompt, indefatigable, ready, and bold, all who have watched his career willingly testify.

Few men have occupied a higher position upon the Pennsylvania bench than Judge Campbell. Regarding the study of law, not merely as a matter of professional duty, but as the investigation of an intricate and beautiful science, he devoted the powers of his fine intellect to it not more as a means of advancement in his profession, than as a matter of taste and subject of intellectual pleasure. With a mind eminently legal in its character—with reasoning powers, active, rapid, and accurate—with that peculiar mental faculty which enables the possessor to disencumber the subject before him of all surplus matter, and follow the correct line of argument without danger of deviation, he united to great research much analytical ability and deep thought. Thus fitted by nature and education for its study—viewing it in this light, and investigating it with this double impulse and purpose, he could not be content with that comparatively superficial knowledge which might have answered the demands of practice, but closely and carefully searched into the anatomy of English and American jurisprudence. Familiar to a remarkable degree with the minutiæ of English history, particularly of those times when law was erected into a system—looking not merely to the prominent features of that system, but to the causes which led to, and the circumstances attendant upon the introduction of those features, he learned to attend less to the letter than to the great purpose and spirit of law. His mind thus early became imbued with those great leading principles which form the only solid basis of legal learning, and are the rules by which alone the correctness of individual decisions can be accurately tested. Making himself acquainted with all important decisions of English and American courts, a remarkably retentive memory enabled him not only to recollect the prominent points decided in each cause, but most usually the detailed history of the case, and the finer and more delicate legal distinctions which were drawn in its progress. This course of study while at the bar, with his clear views of legal philosophy and analogy, enabled him, upon coming to the bench, to decide the difficult questions arising in his courts, not seldom upon unadjudicated points, with great rapidity, and little consultation of authority.

In friendly, social intercourse, he has few superiors. Possessing a fund of information which seems not only to embrace every clime and every subject, but all the prominent personages of every country and every time; a knowledge of the classics, which comprehends not merely the leading authors of Grecian and Roman literature, but the rich and varied fields of learning connected with them;—a fine dramatic taste, and a familiar acquaintance with the leading playwrights;—an acquaintance with history, including not only the narrative of events, but extending to its minor details, and the manners and customs of nations at the different periods of their existence;—a biographical knowledge of the men of Europe and America, which, not confining itself to their history as politicians or men of science, extends to their private lives and characters—with much of the quaint lore of the antiquary;—a fund of anecdote, and a vein of quiet humor seldom surpassed; with rare conversational powers—clothing his ideas in language at once simple and elegant—imparting his information with that absence of pretension which evidences an entire freedom from pedantry—there are very few who do not derive both pleasure and instruction from his society.

With the quiet, easy manner of a gentleman, at home in any company and welcome in all; with that true politeness which, appearing to recognise no difference in men, extends the same dignified courtesy to the humblest and poorest as to the highest and most influential; with that mingled pride and delicacy of character which will flatter the vanity and wound the feelings of no one; plain, unostentatious, and unpretending, it is difficult to know without admiring him, and he is believed to be without a personal enemy. In his intercourse with his fellow men, his frank and cordial address makes for him hosts of friends. His attention to the multiplied details of his office, and his comprehensive and masterly management of its extended and extending operations, are felt and acknowledged in all parts of the country.

The portrait of Judge Campbell which acompanies this sketch, does ample justice to his fine, expressive, and classic countenance.

R. McClelland

SECRETARY OF THE DEPARTMENT OF THE INTERIOR.

Engraved for Biographical Sketches of Eminent Americans.

ROBERT McCLELLAND,

SECRETARY OF THE INTERIOR.

Robert McClelland, of Michigan, is a native of Pennsylvania, and was born at Green Castle, Franklin county. He is a graduate of Dickinson college, and a member of the bar.

After his admission, in 1831, he removed to Pittsburg, and pursued the practice of the law during the year 1832 at that place.

In 1833 he removed to Michigan, and established himself at Monroe in the practice of his profession. The convention assembled for the formation of the constitution of the state of Michigan in 1835, preparatory to her admission into the Union, found him enrolled amongst its most ardent, able, and eloquent members; and in the year 1838, as a member of her legislature, and chairman of several of its most important committees, he was eminently distinguished.

After the political contest which resulted so disastrously to the democratic party in 1840, Mr. McClelland was the acknowledged leader, around whom the faithful few gathered together in the councils of the state, for the vindication of democratic principles.

The confidence of the democracy was justified, the acknowledgment of which was the choice of their champion as Speaker of the popular branch of the State Legislature in the year 1843.

After a warmly contested election in 1843, he was elected to Congress by a majority of about 2500 votes in a district which had given Howard, the whig nominee in 1840, a *whig* majority of 500 over his popular competitor, the Hon. Alpheus Felch. In Congress, as a member of the committee of commerce, his report and advocacy of several important bills attracted the public attention. His re-election to the two succeeding Congresses—the twenty-ninth and thirtieth—manifested the abiding confidence of his constituency; and the personal estimation in which his character and public services were held by his fellow-members of the committee of commerce, of which he was chairman, was pleasingly evinced by their presentation to him of a beautiful cane as a testimonial of official and personal regard. During the ascendency of the whig party in Congress in 1848, he was placed on the committee of Foreign Relations, and had under his peculiar charge the French spoliation bill, and so conducted himself as to command universal respect and esteem.

He left Congress in 1849, and in 1850 became a member of, and was considered to be the leader in the constitutional convention of Michigan. In 1851 he was elected Governor of his adopted State by a majority of more than 7,000, and was re-elected in 1852 by an increased majority, with a popular candidate in the opposition, of over 8,000 votes.

Upon the triumphant restoration of the democratic party, by the almost unexampled unanimity of the public sentiment in the election of General Pierce, with that sagacity which peculiarly distinguishes the President, he selected Governor McClelland for the most interesting and arduous, if not the most important, post in his cabinet, the duties of which he discharges with singular ability and dispatch.

Governor McClelland is a man in whom the elements of true and substantial greatness are happily and harmoniously blended; and it is a fact, no less true than rare, that in none of the many political contests in which he has been engaged, has he ever been personally assailed by his opponents. It has been said, since his entrance into the cabinet, that he is a free-soiler; but how it can be so stated with truth, it is difficult to perceive. On the slavery question, Governor McClelland, when in Congress, like a good and true democrat, represented his constituency; but he never was in favor of any interference with the peculiar institutions of the South, and a more thorough state-rights man than he is not to be found either north or south.

In June, 1850, which was previous to the adoption of the compromise measures by Congress, the members of the Constitutional Convention of Michigan, who were favorable to those measures, held a public meeting and adopted strong resolutions, embracing all the essential features of the compromise acts. Those resolutions were scrutinized and corrected by him, and will meet the sanction and approval of the most fastidious.

In the fall of 1850, he was president of the Democratic State Convention, which adopted strong resolutions, but before they were offered they were submitted to him, and by him examined and cordially approved. Exceedingly strong resolutions in favor of all the compromise measures were likewise offered to the convention which nominated him for governor in 1851;* and in his address to the convention, after having been informed of his nomination, he urged his friends to adopt and cling to those measures as a final settlement of the vexed question of slavery.

In company with General Cass, in 1852, he canvassed the whole State of Michigan, and addressed some twenty or more mass meetings, and always advocated a full and faithful recognition of the constitutionality of the slavery adjustment.

Governor McClelland was a member of the Baltimore Conventions of 1848 and 1852, and was never any more akin to a free-soiler than General Cass, whose right-hand man he was in the contest for the Presidency in 1848.

He is a democrat of the true stamp. He always advocated a strict construction of the constitution, a tariff for revenue only, the independent treasury, and all other prominent democratic measures. He has never yet refused to conform to the usages of the party, but has on all occasions energetically supported democratic principles and the nominees of the party, whether they were of his choice or not.

* The following are the resolutions referred to:

Resolved, That the recent measures of compromise, embracing a settlement of the distracting questions which have disturbed and almost interrupted the business of Congress, and seriously threatened the integrity of the Union itself, were demanded by a fair consideration of the constitutional rights of the various members of the confederacy.

That the democracy of Michigan, pandering to no *isms*, rejecting all alliances with sectional factions, having in view the irrepealable claims of each state in the Union, and yielding only to the demands of the constitution, declare emphatically that the compromise measures stand justified in the eyes of every well-wisher of his country, and should be sustained and executed in all their parts faithfully, fully, and impartially.

Adopted by the Convention of 1851, which nominated Mr. McClelland for Governor.

In Michigan, where he is best known, he is esteemed as a true, consistent, and firm democrat; and no whig, free-soiler, or other opponent in his state will have the hardihood to charge him with any disregard of the constitutional rights of the South, or of any other portion of our free, happy, and glorious Union.

Governor McClelland has now had charge of the Department of the Interior for about a year, and the public may entertain a pretty correct appreciation of the manner in which he directs its dissimilar and complicated affairs. The department exercises appellate powers over all the acts of the Commissioners of the Land, Pension, and Indian Offices, and of the Public Buildings; and partially over those of the Commissioner of Patents, the Inspectors of the Penitentiary of the United States in the District of Columbia, and the accounts of United States marshals, clerks, and attorneys. We may well conceive that the numerous, important, and diverse questions which come under the laws governing these several classes of subjects, offer no bed of roses for the head of the department. It is our opinion that the Interior Department is the most laborious, complicated, and difficult to manage of any. But Governor McClelland, by his untiring industry and application, has brought up much business which had been in arrears since 1847. For a conscientious discharge of duty, inflexible integrity, prudence, and soundness of judgment, he is unsurpassed. He seeks rather to discharge his duties *quietly* and *well*, than with a view to elicit notice or applause. He is very methodical and systematic, and never loses the most perfect control of himself. He is not ambitious, and pays but little attention to private or public complimentary notices.

Earlier in life, Mr. McClelland won a high reputation as a brilliant speaker and powerful debater; to the justice of which the debates in the conventions for the formation and amendment of the constitution of Michigan, which presents throughout the impress of his enlarged statesmanship and democratic spirit, bear ample testimony.

Matured experience, in high public trusts, has elevated his sentiments beyond that meretricious ambition, which has been justly termed "the last infirmity of noble minds," to the purer and loftier aim of usefulness to his country and to mankind. Above no occasion, yet equal to all, whatever may be his future destiny, history has already inscribed his name in the annals of his country, among the imperishable few, as a good, wise, and useful citizen.

As a lawyer, he enjoyed great popularity. He was always disposed to disregard mere quibbles and nice technicalities, and desired to see every case stand or fall on its broad merits. He never resorted to tricks or subterfuges to insure success, and held in contempt all who did. He was, perhaps, more powerful before the jury than the court. Always himself above suspicion, plain and candid, his mere assertion had great weight with jurors in spite of themselves. His oratory is different from any described in the books—it is original and peculiar. He seldom uses quotations, nor often refers to authorities to sustain his argument; indulges in no flights of fancy, or rhetorical flourishes. He comes at once to the subject, and by a masterly statement and thrilling sincerity of manner, removes any prejudices which might have been entertained, and wins the sympathy and judgment of his auditory. There is no mere declamation, no bombast in his speaking. Simplicity is the chief characteristic of the man, and especially is it characteristic of his speaking. There is a plainness and directness about it which makes him always intelligible to the dullest comprehension. His keen and quick perception instantly detects the weak points of his adversary, and they are laid bare as with a dissecting knife, while his unerring sagacity enables him to seize, and set forth prominently, the strong points of his own case. He speaks better than he writes, and speaks with little or no preparation as to what he is to say, relying upon the inspiration of the moment; he warms up and rises in fervor as he progresses with his subject.

Mr. McClelland is distinguished for his firmness and decision of character; and whether in the affairs of life, or in the discharge of his professional duties, for great self-reliance. Yet it must not be inferred that, because these are distinguishing traits of his character, he is obstinate or dogmatic; on the contrary, no one is more ready to receive any counsel which may tend to enlighten his judgment. It is only when that judgment is formed, and when he is fully convinced of its correctness, that he is unswerving and uncompromising.

We cannot conclude this brief sketch without some observation on the private worth of Governor McClelland. We know of no man whose character, in this respect, will bear a severer scrutiny. In all the transactions of life, his conduct is marked by the most scrupulous integrity, and he guards his honor with that sensitive care which has ever kept it far above suspicion. The hearty cordiality of his manner inspires full confidence in the integrity of his heart, and an acquaintance at once desires to become a friend. When that relation is established, he comprehends its duties in the largest extent, and satisfies its demands with a ready, indeed unnecessary generosity.

With great respect

John McLean

Justice of the Supreme Court of the U.S.

Engraved for Biographical Sketches of Eminent [illegible]

HON. JOHN McLEAN,

JUSTICE OF THE SUPREME COURT OF THE UNITED STATES.

A low, vaulted chamber, in the eastern basement of the capitol, having no pretensions to architectural splendor and ornament, is the place where the supreme judicial department of the federal government has its local habitation. There is exercised an authority, bounded in its territorial extent only by the limits of the republic. It embraces among its subjects individuals, tribes, and sovereign states, the operations of the state and federal governments in various departments and relations, and determines rights incident to peace and war. Its judges are called upon sometimes to administer the laws of nations, the laws of the federal republic, the laws of the several states, to expound national treaties, and enforce private contracts. In the variety, importance, and majesty of its jurisdiction, and the wisdom and simplicity of its exercise, the Supreme Court of the United States has no parallel upon earth, and is without example in the history of the world. The stranger in Washington who comes into the presence of this tribunal, and witnesses the grave simplicity and wisdom that distinguishes its proceedings, feels a degree of respect and veneration inspired by no other department of the government. As with deep interest he looks upon the magistrates clothed with such high authority, his eye will rest upon the calm and dignified countenance of Mr. Justice McLean, who now sits in that chamber, the survivor of Marshall and Story, at the right hand of the Chief Justice, the senior judge in commission.

A Judge of the Supreme Court of the United States, Postmaster-General, Commissioner of the General Land-Office, Member of Congress, a Judge of the Supreme Court of his own state—these important stations in the three departments of government, executive, legislative, and judicial, comprise the sphere of Judge McLean's public life. The manner in which they have been filled is distinguished by an ability equaled only by the integrity of his private life; presenting a character useful and worthy of respect in its day and generation, extending by example its influence to all time.

The history of such a life is the history of the country. In the brief space allotted for this sketch can only be traced in outline the path by which, from obscure youth and humble station, Judge McLean has attained the honors of his mature age. And it will thus be seen that, while such distinction is reached by few, the path to it in this republican government is open to all; that to his principles may be ascribed the usefulness and success of his life.

> "Lives of great men all remind us,
> We can make our lives sublime,
> And departing, leave behind us
> Foot-prints on the sands of time."

In Morris county, New-Jersey, on the 11th of March, 1785, John McLean was born. Four years afterwards his father, in humble cir cumstances, with a large family, removed to the western country; settling for a short time, first at Morganstown, Virginia, afterwards on Jessamine, near the town of Nicholasville, Kentucky, from whence he removed, in 1793, to the neighborhood of Mayslick, and finally, in 1799, to that part of the territory northwest of the Ohio River, which now constitutes Warren county, Ohio. He settled upon and cleared a farm in this new country, where, for forty years, and until his death, he resided. His son afterwards owned, and for a long time resided upon, the homestead. The means of education in that country in those days were very limited, and, in the father's condition, the son could not be sent abroad to be educated; but, being sent to school at an early age, he made great proficiency in the elementary branches of education. Laboring on the farm until sixteen years of age, he then received instruction from the Reverend Matthew Wallace and Mr. Stubbs in the languages, with which, by their aid and diligent study, he became well acquainted;—in the mean time, with generous independence, refusing to tax his father's limited means, he by his own labor maintained himself, and defrayed the expenses of his tuition.

Ardent and aspiring, at an early age he resolved to pursue the legal profession. Animated with genuine ambition, dismayed by no difficulties, with firm and determined purpose confiding in his own virtue and industry to overcome all obstacles, he engaged, at the age of eighteen years, to write in the clerk's office of Hamilton county, in Cincinnati, in order to maintain himself by devoting a portion of his time each day to that labor, while pursuing the study of law under the direction of Arthur St. Clair, an eminent counselor, son of the distinguished general of that name, and who had been governor and judge of the Northwest Territory. While supporting himself, he thus acquired, in connection with the principles of legal science, a knowledge of the practical forms of his profession, the details of public business, and formed those methodical and diligent habits that proved of infinite service in his subsequent career. In addition to his other employments he became a member, and took an active part in the discussions, of a debating society in Cincinnati, many of whose members have since attained distinction in the public service. And it may well be doubted whether any mode of instruction more efficient could have been devised for the future lawyer, statesman and judge, than was diligently resorted to for three years by the young aspirant for his own improvement, and to overcome his straitened circumstances and secure his independence.

In the spring of 1807, being then twenty-two years of age, Mr. McLean was married to a lady of amiable manners and great benevolence of character, Miss Rebecca Edwards, daughter of Dr. Edwards, formerly of South Carolina. She was for many years his devoted companion, sharing the struggles of his early life and the honors of his manhood, in her own sphere presiding with judgment and discretion over the cares of a large family.

In the fall of 1807, he was admitted to the bar; and entering upon the practice of law at Lebanon, in Warren county, he soon found himself in the enjoyment of public confidence, and in the receipt of ample professional emoluments.

At the October election in 1812, becoming a candidate to represent in Congress his district, which then included the city of Cincinnati, after an animated contest with two competitors, he was elected by a large majority over both of the opposing candidates. The political principles with which he entered public life, and the manner they were acted upon, in the high and responsible station to which he was now called, have been thus stated: "From his first entrance upon public life, John McLean was identified with the democratic party. He was an ardent supporter of the war, and of the administration of Mr. Madison, yet not a blind advocate of every measure proposed by the party, as the journals of that period will show. His notes were all given in reference to principle. The idea of supporting a dominant party, merely because it was dominant, did not influence his judgment, or withdraw him from the high path of duty which he had marked out for himself. He was well aware, that the association of individuals into parties, was sometimes absolutely necessary to the prosecution and accomplishment of any great public measure. This he supposed was sufficient to induce the members composing them, on any little difference with the majority, to sacrifice their own judgment to that of the greater number, and to distrust their own opinions when they were in contradiction to the general views of the party. But as party was thus to be regarded as itself, only an instrument for the attainment of some great public good, the instrument should not be raised into greater importance than the end, nor any clear and undoubted principle of morality be violated for the sake of adherence to party. Mr. McLean often voted against political friends: yet so highly were both his integrity and judgment estimated, that no one of the democratic party separated himself from him on that account. Nor did his independent course in the smallest degree diminish the weight he had acquired among his own constituents."

Among the measures supported by him, were the tax bills of the extra session at which he first entered Congress. He originated the law to indemnify individuals for property lost in the public service. A resolution instructing the proper committee to inquire into the expediency of giving pensions to the widows of the officers and soldiers who had fallen in their country's service, was introduced by him; and the measure was afterwards sanctioned by Congressional enactment. By an able speech he defended the war measures of the administration; and by the diligent discharge of his duties in respect to the general welfare of the country, and the interests of his people and district, he continued to rise in public estimation. In 1814, he was re-elected to Congress by the unanimous vote of his district, receiving not only every vote cast in the district for representative, but every voter that attended the polls voted for him—a circumstance that has rarely occurred in the political history of any man. His position as a member of the committee of foreign relations and of the public lands, indicates the estimation in which he was held, and his familiarity with the important questions of foreign and domestic policy which were in agitation during the eventful period of his membership. The wide field for public usefulness presented by the representative branch of the national legislature, induced him to decline earnest solicitations to become a candidate for the United States Senate in 1815, at a time when his election was regarded as certain, although he had only attained his thirtieth year, and was therefore barely eligible. He remained in Congress until 1816, when the legislature of Ohio having unanimously elected him a judge of the Supreme Court of that state, he resigned his seat in Congress at the close of the session, and was succeeded as representative of that district by General Harrison.

After his acceptance of the judgeship, and before his resignation, the famous compensation bill was reported, giving to each member of Congress a salary of fifteen hundred dollars a-year, in lieu of the per diem allowance then paid, which was supported by the judge and by the principal members of Congress of both political parties. He was on the committee that reported the bill; and being convinced that it was a measure eminently calculated to advance the public service, he voted for it, believing that it would shorten the sessions of Congress, give it a more business character, and greatly lessen the public expenditure. Under this law, no useless discussions would have been tolerated, and the business before Congress would have been promptly dispatched. But the law was perverted, and its effects misrepresented by selfish aspirants, so that at the next session it was repealed, and the present law, giving eight dollars per day, and eight dollars for every twenty miles travel, was passed. Under the salary system, few members would have consented to remain in session longer than was necessary to act on the business before them. The contingent expenses of Congress would have been one-third less than they now are, and the annual pay of the members would have been proportionably reduced: at the same time, they would have been better paid for the time spent in legislation. But the most desirable feature in the reform would have been found in the increasing dignity and business character of the body.

Judge McLean remained six years upon the Supreme Bench of Ohio, serving the state with great advantage to its jurisprudence, and evincing those professional attainments and judicial qualities that have since distinguished his present station. In the summer of 1822, he was appointed Commissioner of the General Land Office by President Monroe; and in July, 1823, he became Postmaster-General.

The administration of the General Post-Office, in the condition it then was, presented so little for an ambitious man of reputation to hope for, and so much to dread, that his friends earnestly endeavored to dissuade him from accepting the appointment. Disordered arrangements, depressed finances, arduous duties, public complaints and distrust, not unmingled with groundless abuse and calumny, presented a field where it was generally thought no reputation could be won. But confiding in his own industry and ability, and relying with confidence upon the virtue and intelligence of the people properly to estimate devotion to their service, Judge McLean resolved to undertake the hazard of the office. Order and economy enforced, finances improved and credit restored, regularity and dispatch of the mail, intercourse extended, and commercial correspondence carried on with ease, celerity, and security before unknown, soon manifested the application of his vigorous mind and methodical habits to the complicated affairs of the Post-office department. Devoting his personal attention to all the details of business, guarding against fraud and corruption in the making and execution of contracts, promptly dismissing unfaithful and inefficient contractors, agents, and postmasters, superintending all the correspondence, and acting upon all appointments and complaints, his administration of this department was rewarded with unexampled success and public confidence. By a nearly unanimous vote of the Senate and House, the Postmaster-General's salary was increased from four to six thousand dollars. Those who from motives of policy opposed the measure, did so with reluctance; and John Randolph said the salary was for the officer and not for the office, and that he would vote for the bill if the law should be made to expire when Judge McLean left the office.

The distribution of the public patronage of his department exhibited in another respect his qualities as an executive officer, and manifested the rule of action that has always marked his character. The principle upon which executive patronage should be distributed, has been one of the most important questions in this government, and has presented the widest variation between the profession and practice of individuals and parties. In the administration of the Post-office department by Judge McLean, an example was presented in strict consistence with sound principles of republican government, and just party organization. "During the whole time that the affairs of the department were administered by the judge, he had necessarily a difficult part to act. The country was divided into two great parties, animated by the most determined spirit of rivalry, and each bent on advancing itself to the lead of public affairs. A question was now started, whether it was proper to make political opinions the test of qualification for office. Such a principle had been occasionally acted upon during preceding periods of our history; but so rarely, as to constitute the exception, rather than the rule. It had never become the settled and systematic course of conduct of any public officer. Doubtless every one is bound to concede something to the temper and opinions of the party to which he belongs, otherwise party would be an association without any connecting bond of alliance. But no man is permitted to infringe any one of the great rules of morality and justice, for the sake of subserving the interests of his party. It cannot be too often repeated, nor too strongly impressed upon the public men of America, that nothing is easier than to reconcile these two apparently conflicting views. The meaning of party, is an association of men for the purpose of advancing the public interests. Men thrown together indiscriminately, without any common bond of alliance, would be able to achieve nothing great and valuable; while united together, to lend each other mutual support and assistance, they are able to surmount the greatest obstacles, and to accomplish the most important ends. This is the true notion of party. It imports combined action; but does not imply any departure from the great principles of truth and honesty. So long as the structure of the human mind is so varied in different individuals, there will always be a wide scope for diversity of opinion as to public measures; but no foundation is yet laid in the human mind for any material difference of opinion, as to what constitutes the great rule of justice.

"The course which was pursued by Judge McLean, was marked by the greatest wisdom and moderation. Believing that every public officer holds his office in trust for the people, he determined to be influenced by no other principle in the discharge of his public duties, than a faithful performance of the trust committed to him. No individual was removed from office by him, on account of his political opinions. In making appointments where the claims and qualifications of persons were equal, and at the same time one was known to be friendly to the administration, he felt himself bound to appoint the one who was his friend. But when persons were recommended to office, it was not the practice to name, as a recommendation, that they had been or were warm supporters of the dominant power. In all such cases, the man who was believed to be the best qualified was selected by the department."

Having illustrated his principles and character in private and professional life, in legislative, judicial and executive functions, Judge McLean was now called to exercise his capacity and attainments in the full maturity of their strength, in the highest judicial station. By the appointment of General Jackson in 1829, he was placed upon the Bench of the Supreme Court of the United States, having declined the War and Navy departments, which were tendered to him. The circumstances that accompanied this appointment evincing the confidential relations that existed between General Jackson and Judge McLean, notwithstanding their different sentiments upon some principles of public policy, are interesting and highly creditable to both parties. They have been thus related:

"On the arrival of General Jackson, after his election to the presidency, and when he was about selecting the members of his cabinet, Judge McLean was sent for to ascertain whether he was willing to remain at Washington. General Jackson having stated the object of the interview, the judge remarked, that he was desirous to explain the line of conduct he had hitherto pursued: observing, that the general might have received the impression from some of the public prints, that the Postmaster-General had used the patronage of his office for the purpose of advancing the general's election; but he wished him to understand, that no such thing had been done—and that had he pursued such a course, he would deem himself unworthy of the President's confidence, or that of any other honorable man. But that he was bound in candor to say, should he remain in office, he would not deviate in any respect from the course he had pursued under Mr. Adams; that in all he had done he had looked with a single eye to the public interest, and that the same motives would govern his future action; that no power, which could be brought to bear upon him, would change his purpose. The general replied with warm expressions of regard and confidence, and wished him to remain in the post-office department. He at the same time expressed regret, that circumstances did not enable him to offer the judge the treasury department. The judge replied, that having held office under the late administration, he was delicately situated, and required no distinction in his organization; that he would remain in the post-office department on the terms stated, or retire, as might be deemed proper." It was well here to remark, that the postmaster-general was not a member of the cabinet, until he was made so by General Jackson. Some of the personal friends of the judge, who had been designated for the cabinet, fearing that his course in the post-office department might not harmonize with the one which the members of the cabinet felt themselves bound to take, had conversations with him on the subject: and finding his purpose not to be changed, a seat on the Supreme Bench was offered to him, which he accepted, and to which he was immediately nominated.

Judge McLean had received so large a share of public confidence in political life, and believing the people would sustain a public servant who honestly devoted his time and abilities to their service, that he left the department with great reluctance. He desired, above all things earthly, to see this great and glorious experiment of free government carried out in its true spirit. And this, he doubted not, would secure through all time to come, unbounded prosperity and happiness to those who were under its jurisdiction; and that its moral power would so operate upon the civilized world, sooner or later, as to overturn the thrones of despotism, and introduce in every nation a national liberty.

At the January term, 1830, Judge McLean entered upon his duties as a judge of the Supreme Court of the United States. There is, perhaps, no station which calls into exercise, to a greater degree, the highest faculties of the human intellect. In that tribunal must be discussed not only points of judicial learning, but theoretic and practical questions of art, science and government frequently arise, their decision involving the present and future rights and interests of citizens and of states, the prosperity of commerce, the extent of legislative and executive powers, the stability of republican principles, and the progress of mankind towards peace and happiness. Judge McLean's eminent fitness for that station has been manifested by twenty-two years' service upon the Supreme Bench, in which period the jurisprudence of the country has been enriched by the diligent labors of his energetic and cultivated mind. By his early habits of labor and industry, his intellect was trained and his body inured to undergo exhaustion and fatigue greater than is imposed upon any other department of the government. Upon questions of commerce and constitutional law, his opinions have been distinguished; evincing great powers of reasoning and investigation, they manifest a clear perception of the principles upon which the federal government was established, a profound veneration of their wisdom, and an inflexible firmness in their support.

The duties of the judges of the Supreme Court requiring the exercise of their functions not only in term at the capitol, but in their respective circuits, they may exercise an important influence upon the bar and upon the character of state jurisprudence. In this respect the influence of Judge McLean has been sensibly felt. His courtesy and patient attention to counsel, the dignity of his demeanor, and the uprightness of his conduct upon the bench and in private life, observed by the lawyers assembled at the state capitals, and by intelligent jurors and witnesses, have afforded an example which, throughout his circuit, is held in high estimation. Some of his charges to grand juries in the crises of important events, are regarded as the most able and eloquent expositions of the rights and duties of American citizens amongst themselves towards foreign nations and other states. The reports of the Supreme Court of the United States, and the reports of his decisions upon the circuit, form a monument of judicial fame, for which the honors awarded to the chief magistrate of the republic would be a free exchange.

The honorary degree of Doctor of Laws has been conferred upon Judge McLean by Cambridge University, the Wesleyan University, and by several other colleges and institutions of learning in the western and southwestern states.

In December, 1840, the judge suffered the severest affliction to which any man can be subjected, in the loss of the companion of his youth and the mother of his children. She died as she had lived, an example of virtue and the triumphs of religion. In 1843, he married Mrs. Sarah Bella Garrard, daughter of Israel Ludlow, Esq., one of the founders of Cincinnati, a lady extensively known and admired for the graces of her person, the charm of her manners, and the accomplishments of her refined and cultivated intellect.

Judge McLean is tall and well-proportioned in person, his appearance indicating great vigor of body and intellectual energy. His habits of life have always been simple and unostentatious. Cheerful in temper, frank in manners, instructive and eloquent in conversation, he possesses, in rare degree, the faculty of inspiring confidence and warm attachment towards him in those who come within his influence, especially in young members of the bar, towards whom his kindness and courtesy has always been extended. A professor of the Christian religion, he has sought to regulate his public and private life in strict consistence with his faith; by diligence, justice, and charity, showing forth the consistence of religious principles and profession with the duties of a citizen, a lawyer, a statesman and a judge.

Very respectfully
Your obedt
R C Grier

Justice of the Supreme Court of the U.S.

HON. ROBERT C. GRIER,

JUSTICE OF THE SUPREME COURT OF THE UNITED STATES.

The life of a professional or literary man seldom exhibits any of those striking incidents that seize upon public feeling, and fix attention upon himself. His character is generally made up of the aggregate of the qualities and qualifications he may possess, as these may be elicited by the exercise of the duties of his vocation, or the particular profession to which he may belong. The subject of this brief notice may not form an exception to this general rule. His life has been one of hard study from his youth, and, since maturity, of laborious professional duty in the several relations in which he has been placed; and the high place to which he has attained is evidence that these qualities afford the means of distinction under a system of government in which the places of honor are open to all who may be found worthy of them.

Robert Cooper Grier was born March 5th, 1794, in Cumberland county, Pennsylvania, where his father, the Rev. Isaac Grier, at that time resided: his mother was the daughter of the Rev. Robert Cooper, of the same county, both of the Presbyterian Church. His father removed from Cumberland to Lycoming county, in the same state, in the fall of 1794, where he bought a farm, and built a house on it, a little below the mouth of Pine Creek, on the west bank of the Susquehanna River. While resident there, he preached to three congregations for a very small compensation, deriving the means of his support mainly from a grammar-school which he taught, and the proceeds of his farm. He was a very superior Greek and Latin scholar, and every way competent as an instructor in those languages. And his amiable and excellent character, his benevolence and faithfulness as a pastor, gained for him the affections of all who knew him. Few men in a like sphere have been more beloved; and the many excellencies of the father's character were not lost upon the son. The latter, at the age of six years, began to learn Latin under the instructions of his father, and, by the time he had reached his twelfth year, had mastered the usual course of Latin and Greek as they were then taught in ordinary schools. He continued his studies, under his father's direction, till 1811, when he went to Dickenson College, and entered the junior class half advanced. In the mean time, in 1806 his father had removed to Northumberland, Pa., having been invited to take charge of the academy at that place; and there also he served three congregations in his capacity of clergyman, but supporting his family mainly, as formerly, by the revenue derived from his labors as a teacher. His method of conducting the academy did honor to his talents. It grew under his care into a highly respectable establishment, and obtained a high character in that district of country. This reputation, and the thoroughness of the course of instruction pursued, was the means of elevating the academy into a college, under an ample charter, with power to confer degrees in the usual form in like institutions. This enlargement called for more of the *machinery* of education than the institution had before possessed; and the library of a celebrated professor, who had lived the latter part of his life in Northumberland, and not long before had died there, together with his philosophical apparatus, were procured for the college.

In the meantime, the subject of this notice continued at Dickenson College. His aptitude for the languages and early instruction had placed him far ahead of all competitors in that branch. He was so thoroughly master of the Latin that he could write it with facility, perhaps as well as his mother tongue; and, though indifferent to, and never troubling himself about, college honors, his superior ability and acquirements were not questioned. His instructor in chemistry was Doctor Cooper, formerly a judge in the interior of Pennsylvania, then Professor of Chemistry in Dickenson College, and afterwards President of Columbia College, South Carolina, whither he had been invited by the state, and known throughout the country for his extensive literary and scientific attainments, and with whom our student was always a favorite. He graduated at Dickenson in 1812, but taught grammar-school in the college till 1813, when he returned to Northumberland to aid his father in his college duties, now become onerous by the addition of numerous students, and the increasing duties of the enlarged institution.

Shortly after this, his father's health began to fail. He became dyspeptic, and this disease continued to enfeeble and distress him up to the period of his death, which occurred in 1815. And few men have lived more beloved, or died more lamented.

His virtues and many excellencies of character did not perish; they left their impress long on the community in which he had lived, and have descended upon his son—a goodly inheritance, and one that passeth not away.

The well-known acquirements of the son pointed to him, young as he then was, (not twenty years of age,) as the successor of the father, and he was accordingly, soon after the death of the former, appointed principal of the college; and in this new situation the extent and variety of his duties go to show how much may be accomplished where resolution and will are combined with ability. He graduated the classes, delivered lectures on chemistry, taught astronomy and mathematics, Greek and Latin, and studied law, all at the same time.

His law instructor was Charles Hall, Esq., late of Sunbury, Northumberland county, a gentleman eminent in the profession, under whom he was admitted to the bar in 1817, and commenced practice the same year.

His professional career, which has since proved so successful, commenced in Bloomsburg, Columbia county, Pennsylvania. There he continued, however, but a short time, for we find him settled in Danville, in the same county, in 1818. Here his practice rapidly increased, and was soon extended to four or five of the surrounding counties, and there he continued till he was appointed, by Governor Wolf, President Judge of the District Court of Alleghany county.

And here it may not be improper to state certain events, very well known and justly appreciated in the place and neighborhood where they took place, and which evince the excellent qualities of heart of the subject of our note. At his father's death, he found himself the oldest of many brothers and sisters, including himself, eleven in number, most of them young and helpless; and they, together with his widowed mother, were entirely dependent upon him for their support. Well and faithfully did he perform the duties that this condition of things called for. He possessed but little of this world's goods, but he had health, energy, talent, and a profession; but he bent himself to the task, and with these materials, fairly brought into requisition under the guidance of a sound and affectionate heart and a willing mind, he overcame all difficulty. His brothers were well and liberally educated, and settled in business or professions. His sisters lived with him till they were married; and his mother, till she died. As a son and brother, as well as in all subsequently formed domestic relations, he has been distinguished by the kindest and tenderest affections; and no man is more beloved by his family and friends. If it be true that the recollection of kind and benevolent actions warms the heart into peace with itself, then may our friend well rejoice in the past, and look to the future in the thankfulness of hope.

But to our narrative. His brothers and sisters being all married and settled in life, he had leisure to look out for himself; and in the year 1829, he married Miss Isabella Rose, the daughter of John Rose, Esq., a native of Scotland, who emigrated to this country in 1798. Mr. Rose had been admitted to the bar in Europe, but never practised, or sought practice here. He was a gentleman of education and accomplishments, and possessed of considerable estate. He bought a beautifully-situated farm on the banks of the Lycoming Creek, about two miles above Williamsport, in Lycoming county, upon which he resided till his death, and which now belongs to Judge Grier. This stream is celebrated for the fine trout with which it abounds, some distance from its mouth. And this we mention more particularly, as the judge makes an annual excursion to his farm and fishing-ground, to enjoy his favorite vocation of trout-fishing. He early became a disciple of Isaac Walton, and is faithful to his preceptor to this day. Nothing is suffered to interfere with this excursion: and when the month of June arrives, he is sure to find his way to the creek, with a few select companions, and all the necessary apparatus for catching and cooking his favorite fish, together with all manner of generous accompaniments to give zest to the luxury. This fishing-ground is in the midst of the eastern ridges of the Alleghany Mountains, into which the stream penetrates, and is surrounded with dense forests in their primitive state. The invigorating air of the woods, the beauty and wildness of the scenery, contrasted with that to which he is accustomed, the continued exercise and pleasure of the sport, sometimes not without adventure, all have their charm. And the judge returns to his professional duties, somewhat sunburned and weatherbeaten, to be sure, but with recovered powers, renovated frame, and clear head, ready for another year of labor.

His appointment to the District Court of Alleghany county was made May 4th, 1838. He removed to Pittsburgh in October of the same year, and resided in Alleghany City till September, 1848, when he removed to Philadelphia, where he continues to reside.

On the 4th of August, 1846, he was nominated, by President Polk, one of the Justices of the Supreme Court of the United States, in the place of Judge Baldwin, deceased, and was unanimously confirmed by the Senate the next day.

The professional career of Judge Grier, while at the bar, was marked by high integrity of purpose, and fidelity to his client, qualities not unusual in the profession; but with him there was a benevolence not so universal, and generosity towards those who sought his services with but limited means of remuneration, that procured him many clients of this description; and for many has he gone through with repeated and arduous conflicts, without money and without price.

In the conducting of his case, he was not apt to trouble himself much about its mere technicalities, and despised all the tricks and catches of the law; he regarded mainly the principles involved in it, and arguing it upon this basis, his views were clear and logical, and always delivered with great distinctness and force.

While presiding in the District Court at Pittsburgh, he had the confidence of all the bar, which was one of the ablest in the state. There was a deference paid to his decisions highly honorable, and an attachment to himself personally, not often found to exist in the same degree between the bar and the bench. If the cause before him had merits, its advocate had nothing to fear; if doubtfal, he was sure of a fair and candid hearing; but if without merits, or if tinctured with fraud, it behooved him to take care of his case, for he was sure of neither aid nor quarter from the court.

With the jury, his charge was everything: they had entire confidence in his integrity and learning, and knew that he only aimed to arrive at justice. Their verdict was responsive to his instructions. And when exception was taken to his charge or opinion, nothing was withheld by selfish regard to pride of opinion, or petty doubt as to the unnecessary action of a higher tribunal. His view of the law was fairly stated, and sent up as delivered, without addition or diminution, upon its own merits to stand or fall. All men are liable to err, but he who feels the consciousness of power within himself, fears not, but rather desires the examination of his opinions by those who may have the power, together with the responsibility, of sustaining or reversing them. Every judicial opinion affects the property, the reputation, or the person of some one, to a greater or less extent; and a faithful judge would rather rejoice in the detection of his error, than that it should be suffered to exist to the injury of another.

Since the elevation of Judge Grier to the Supreme Court, his judicial reputation has become the common property of the country, and is well established. His discussions bear testimony to this, and these are in the hands of every professional man. They disclose extensive learning and research, and a persevering seeking of the principle lying at the basis of the particular point under discussion—and this discovered, it is never lost sight of; and the conclusion arrived at is pronounced with the boldness of a fearless spirit, regardless of all consequences, save the one aim of bringing the truth to light, and giving effect to the law. His argument will stand the test of strict scrutiny; is clear in its statements and details, marked, perhaps, more by the qualities of common-sense, clearness and strength, than by any effort after ornament, though by no means deficient in illustration, which is readily supplied by h s well-stored mind. The works which contain the evidence of Judge Grier's judicial reputation are accessible to every one—an examination of these would swell this notice far beyond the limits assigned to it, and would require more time and ability than the writer has to bestow. He leaves it, therefore, to abler hands.

His elevation to the distinguished place he now holds, has worked no alteration in the MAN. The same modest worth that marked his youth and maturity, continues to adorn his riper years. The same kindness of disposition to all, the same attachment to friends, and affection for those dependent upon him: a lover of his country, and, of the very necessity of his nature, a religious man, and therefore a Christian—long a member of the church in the principles of which he was educated, and some time participating in its government—but liberal in his views, regarding the spirit rather than the letter of his creed. Happy in his domestic relations, in the affections of an amiable and excellent wife, in the love of his children, in the attachment of his many friends, and highly honored, as he is, by his country—his life affords an example of the triumph of right principles, unshrinking integrity, persevering industry, and fidelity to truth and to himself, over difficulties of formidable character, and from which a mind of less energy would have shrunk.

> "Heaven does with us as we with torches do,
> Not light them for ourselves: for if our virtues
> Did not go forth of us, 'twere all the same
> As if we had them not."

J. Catron.

Justice of the Supreme Court of the U. S.

Eng^d for Biographical Sketches of Eminent Americans

BIOGRAPHICAL LETTER FROM JUSTICE CATRON.

OF THE SUPREME COURT OF THE UNITED STATES.

DEAR SIR,—Some days since I received your letter of the 15th instant, in which you express a desire to publish in your magazine a sketch of my life, with a portrait, &c.

For your kindness and good opinion, be pleased to accept my thanks. I do not believe there is a man living who could give you any tolerable account of my early life, except myself; and when the incidents were narrated, they would only prove, what Campbell says of Lord Mansfield—that when he came up from Scotland to Westminister School on a Highland pony, the chances were a billion to one against his ever being Chief Justice: and I can safely say, that quite as many chances stood in the way of my being a Supreme Judge, when of the same age, as was his Lordship at the time he wended his solitary way south, with his pony as his sole companion. Your readers would only learn that I had been reared on a farm, and been flogged through the common schools in Western Virginia and Kentucky, and then had had the advantages of such academies as the western country afforded;* humble enough in all conscience, and where little else than Latin, and the lower mathematics, was added to the common school training; that with this amount of ac-

---

* As I am one of the few who have any recollection left of these schools, it may not be out of place to give some account of them. They usually consisted of a single teacher, and he a clergyman, having occasionally an assistant. Six days in the week were devoted to teaching; nor were the schools crowded with pupils. At the head of this description of teachers stood James Priestley, an Englishman, and nephew to Doctor Joseph Priestley. He first taught at Bairdstown, Kentucky; then at Danville, and concluded his labors at Nashville, Tennessee, where his academy was denominated Cumberland College. I believe he was an Eaton man. His scholars commenced and ended with the dead languages, in which this teacher greatly excelled. Other branches were taught of course; but Latin was the great foundation laid in by his pupils; in this they were trained as if in spans and yokes, for four years at the least. How it happened that he turned out so many good writers and speakers, I never could tell; but certainly, for the number taught, both in Kentucky and Tennessee, the proportion of successful men was remarkably great.

Others followed the same plan. I was taught by the Rev. James Witherspoon, a Presbyterian clergyman, who had been a professor of languages. He also relied on the dead languages as the main basis of education; was well qualified to teach them, and could have preached in Latin as well as English. A distinguished lawyer and friend advised me to study English well, and not waste so much time on that which he said all lawyers forgot very soon. It struck me as sound advice, and I named to my teacher that I wished to study the English grammar. He replied that the thing was unheard of; that to be a good Latin scholar was to be a good English one; furthermore, that he had never opened an English grammar. But I insisted, and we commenced together with Murray's grammar and key. It took me some three weeks to memorize the necessary parts, and when the time came for an effort at parsing, I took it for granted that I was ahead of my teacher; but in this I found myself greatly mistaken. We had the edition of Murray from which he had rejected the objective case. This, Mr. W. declared, was a mistake—saying Murray

quired knowledge, I read history, novels, and poetry; grounded myself well, *as I thought*, in Virginia politics; that I read everything that came to hand as it came—Fielding, Smollet, Sterne, Goldsmith, and up through Tom Paine, Hume and Gibbon. Everything, or nearly so, then to be had in the country, of history, ancient and modern, was read, and much of it, with a devouring appetite. Prester John, Peter the Hermit, Richard and Saladin, Falstaff and Frederick, were all jumbled up together. It is due, however, to say, that preparatory to taking up Blackstone, I carefully re-read Hume's History of England, with Smollet's and Bisset's continuations; Robertson's Charles the Fifth, and also Gibbon's Decline and Fall; and made extensive notes on each, which I thought exceedingly valuable at the time. They were on large foolscap, bound in pasteboard, and all told were, when packed on each other, two-thirds as high as a table: nor did I doubt that *my condensed* Gibbon would go forth one day to the world in print; nor do I now remember at what time it was used to kindle the office fire; but this was its fate.* With my old friends, Pope, Shakspeare and Sterne, I had to act, as I have often done since with my snuff-box—hide them from myself. But just then the veritable History of New-York, by Diedrich Knickerbocker, made its appearance amongst us young men of the West, which I did not attempt to resist then, nor at any time afterwards. And it is well I did not, for the matchless humor of that production has stood me in hand many times before juries, who got into the dangerous mood of an inclination to cry, when the clear interest of my client was that they should laugh. Most lawyers know the immi-

---

might as well have stricken out the corresponding accusative from the Latin grammar; and he inserted the rejected case with his pen. When we set about parsing he had no difficulty whatever; and showed the difference between the English and Latin structures of the respective languages with an ease wholly incomprehensible to me, then or since. And I am compelled to admit, that good English scholars may be made without reading English grammar; but why it is so, I do not know. Certain it is, that Priestley's scholars were equal to any ever educated in the western country; and he would as soon have thought of making "Paine's Age of Reason" a class-book as Murray's Grammar.

Several of these schools were denominated colleges, but they were conducted alike, high and low. Some of our young mer were sent to Princeton, Yale and Harvard, and returned with great prospects, as they and their friends supposed, but success did not attend them; they were no match for those educated at home; and parents were taught the important truth, that where a boy is expected to spend his after life, and to succeed as a man, there he should be educated—if it can be done; so that a knowledge of men, and the habits of the people among whom he is to live and act, may be acquired as his scholastic learning progresses. One educated abroad, may return with stringent ideas of a wise economy, and a well-stored mind from books; his theories may be very good; but in nine instances among ten, he is a dissatisfied man, that complains of everything at home, and who finds a carping temper to be a sorry handmaid in the war of life.

* All men of experience must be aware, that the style of banter indulged in here, means more than merely to amuse; that its object is to present an attractive picture of the means employed by a vigorous and ambitious youth to become an intelligent man under circumstances where he had to rely, for his course of reading and study, almost exclusively on his own judgment, unguided by a single man of general reading and matured scholarship. Placed in his circumstances, few would have done better, or judged more wisely, and thousands would have done worse. He had to read much, to the end, of learning where to begin and how to study: nor

nent peril a felon is in, when a jury begins to be sorrowful over his case, and when burglary, arson, robbery, forging bank-notes, or passing them, and several other crimes, not now amounting to much, were capital adroit shifts to evade the pithy sentence of "Sus. per Col.," were deemed allowable.

The Bible, being the common reader of my early schools, of course I knew almost by memory. Of geography I learned more than most men, and know more now. With this confused mass of self-taught knowledge, I commenced to read law in April, 1812, in the State of Tennessee. Up to this date, I had never been sick a day, or hour, and had a frame rarely excelled; one that could bear ardent and rigorous application for sixteen hours in the day, and which was well tried for about four years at something like this rate. Late in 1815, I tried my chances at the bar, and succeeded; certainly in the main chance of getting fees; but then I had a good deal of worldly experience, and availed myself of the cases in court, throughout a heavy circuit, of a retiring brother lawyer and friend who was elected to Congress. To his business I attended, taking the unpaid fees; and as he had a side in almost every important cause, "I run from the score" at the start, and which my elder brethren liberally applied for a year or two. Having served a campaign under General Jackson, and brought home some army popularity, the legislature of Tennessee elected me attorney for the government in my circuit, when my law license had the sand on it. The courts were full of indictments for crimes, from murder down. Here I had to fight the battle, single and alone, and to work day and night. No man ever worked much harder, I think; my circuit judge was an

---

were his labors greatly wasted on this first confused effort. As his mind enlarged, and the prospect lighted up and widened, he discovered, day by day, that his knowledge was in confusion; a compound of facts and fictions that needed systematic adjustment; that his books must be read over again in classes and each class by itself; beginning with the more solid, and concluding the regular and steady course with the lighter works: and in doing this, great advantage was derived from the first reading. A hundred pages as an ordinary task could be gone through in the day, with a review in the evening of leading portions on which the narrative was founded; and then, too, the day's work was abridged on paper, when the mind was heated up to a high state of vigor, and the composition aided by an employment of the author's language and style, which naturally on that occasion excluded all others. Every reader of sound experience knows that so much cannot be accomplished by any young man on first reading a book.

Much has been said to the prejudice of Gibbon's History of the Decline and Fall of the Roman Empire, because of its supposed tendency to imbue the young mind with ideas of infidelity to the Christian religion. When I read this author twice, and after a fashion abridged his matter, my mind was as impressible as the wide do main of new snow that now lies before me; (*) I believed him to be the greatest historian of his nation, if not the first the world had produced. He had my unlimited confidence; and yet, no one impression was made on me that he questioned the truths of Christianity; and when, long after, I heard him charged with infidelity, and chapters of his history referred to, for evidence of the fact, these chapters were re-examined and studied, subject to the criticisms of clergymen who aided me; and still I feel confident that Gibbon is only misunderstood—that his narrative of facts, detailing violent contests among the ancient Fathers, and in councils of the church, have been attributed to him as opinions of his own, which amounted to an infidel creed.

(*) Written at the Capitol, 24th Dec., 1851.

excellent criminal lawyer, and being partly Scotch, always stood firmly by the state, and leaned *strongly* against the culprit: so that I got on very well; but often with an arrogance that would have done credit to Castlereagh, for blundering in my law, certainly, if not bad grammar. Like his lordship, I was given to white waistcoats and small clothes, and drew pretty largely on the adventitious aids furnished by the tailor.

The lawyers then traveled the circuit from county to county, usually of a Sunday. Each man that was well appointed, carried pistols and holsters, and a negro waiter with a large portmanteau behind him. All went on horseback. The pistols were carried, not to shoot thieves and robbers, but to fight each other, if by any chance a quarrel was hatched up, furnishing occasion for a duel, then a very favorite amusement and liberally indulged in—and the attorney-general for the circuit was expected to be, and always was, prepared for such a contingency. He managed to keep from fighting, however. His equipments were of the best, with a led third horse now and then for the sake of parade. Many are the anecdotes I could furnish of nights on the roadside, at country taverns, where the corps of lawyers halted short of the county town, and made as free with whisky punch and empty bottles as did our Irish brethren at a Galway assize about the same time: nor were games at cards overlooked. But the law of the circuit was, that no duel should come of a brawl on these occasions; if any one happened to suffer from a smashed bottle, he took it and made up on the spot.

One station I filled when at the bar, amounting to almost a monopoly; it was that of drawing bills of exception. As a writ of error lay in all cases, civil and criminal, on a refusal to grant a new trial, often the entire facts had to appear with the judge's charge on them. We then took few notes of evidence, having to do more in a day than could be done in a week, if all that witnesses said was tediously written out as the trial progressed. The trial being ended, then the exceptions were required at once; perhaps on the last day of the term. The writing was always done at the bar, and in the confusion of business. So adroit did I become by constant practice, that I could for hours write down and detail what every witness had deposed, as little annoyed by bustle and noise as if entirely alone, being so utterly absorbed as not to know what was going on. But usually on ending the work, found a leg asleep, and sometimes came down, exceptions in hand, just when "please your honor" had come out on the sound leg, and a shift was made to the numb one.

I defended in many criminal cases after I removed to Nashville; was in the defence very generally in the commercial causes; had much to do with chancery practice, and actions of ejectment, and was decidedly famous for enforcing the seven years' act of limitations in real actions; and, after divers defeats and rugged contests, had my revenge by entire success; not so much because of any merit of mine, but for the controlling fact, that John Haywood was the leading judge in the Court of Errors, and who had been a champion on my side of the question for many years before he went on the bench; and presently William L. Brown removed to Nashville, and he, too, was enthusiastic on the same side. This gentleman was of my own age, and by far the ablest legal debater then at the bar; but his frame was too weak for his great volume of brain; he fell into spasms by over-exertion, and died.

These are rough details, that will do little credit to one in so grave a place as I now fill, and especially not in the cities at this day. In the days of Spencer, Kent and Thompson, they would have been understood; they set out under similar auspices, and believed that vigor and practical sense came of circuit practice and experience. That the fortunes of such men as Jackson, Clay, Polk and Benton, and five hundred others in the West, depended on knowledge of men and things thus acquired, I personally know; nor could John Marshall, William Pinkney, or Daniel Webster, have succeeded much without it.

I went to Nashville, (where I have resided since) at the end of the year 1818. In March, 1819, the town and country were overwhelmed with misfortunes in trade, and a general bankruptcy, not known before or since in that country. By the end of that year, the courts had two thousand causes in them at the least, and I had more business than I could do in the town itself, and rarely left it. My success, professionally, was all that could be desired, and I had far more character than I deserved, owing mainly to uncommon capacity for labor, and much ambition to excel *competitors*. The Nashville bar was at that time inferior to none in the United States in contests involving conflicting titles to lands; and possessed uncommon ability in most departments of their profession. The action of ejectment had drawn them there.

In December, 1824, I was elected by the legislature one of the Supreme Judges of the State, which office I held until 1836, having been then beaten and turned out on a new election, under the amended constitution adopted by Tennessee in that year. I had acted as Chief Justice for some six years before I was superseded. Of the Tennessee decisions, whilst I was on the bench, nothing need be said, as they are all reported in the volumes of Mr. Yerger.

The old pastime of dueling was overthrown by striking a lawyer from the rolls, in the case of Smith *vs.* The State, (1 *Yerg.* 228,) in which I delivered the opinion, and set forth my circuit experience; and for which homily to my brethren, I was scorched with many a racy sarcasm; such as, that a sinner who had carried blank challenges in the crown of his hat, and slept with his pistols under his head, was a very proper man to turn saint and lecturer, to put down a vice he so well understood in all its bearings. But as we have not had a duel since, nor a challenge, so far as I know, I still wear the laurels coming of the good advice so unscrupulously set forth to my brethren.

On the 4th of March, 1837, I was nominated to the Senate by President Jackson as a Judge of the Supreme Court of the United States, where I have had some character as being familiar with the laws applicable to cases involving conflicting titles to western and southern lands.

As to my mode of speaking at the bar, I have no very exact recollection. It was not methodical, tolerably fluent, sometimes stormy, and often sarcastic, which habit cost me rather dear on one or two occasions. One thing I recollect very well, that, after being on the bench twelve years, and then attempting to speak in court, I was as much embarrassed as at the outset; and under an obvious necessity of learning the art over again, if I intended to employ it, which I never did.

After I was a lawyer, and a successful one, I cast about me for a permanent place of residence, taking a range from New-Orleans to Baltimore, and Harrisburg, Pennsylvania; and, in the end, sat down where I felt certain of success, where good fortune attended me, as it has throughout, from early manhood up.

I never was a candidate for any political place, nor held any office, except those above referred to, of solicitor and judge. For many years past, I could not have been elected to anything by the people. With the floating masses I had nothing in common: I punished many of them for crimes, and always severely. They feared and disliked me. Among the great mass of property-owners, thousands have been alienated by decisions adverse to their interests. The losing party naturally dislikes the judge who decides against him, and his family and friends take sides; whereas, the party that wins, and all connected with him, promulge aloud, that no judge, not corrupt, or a dunce, could have decided otherwise; and so it falls out that half of a neighborhood, for a single decision, turn enemies, and the other half do not stand by the judge as friends. This process will pervade a whole country in a dozen or twenty years, when, during the time, the same judge has made thousands of decisions affecting almost every interest and every influential family in the community. A judge may have great cogency and influence with very many of the most intelligent class; but if he be a stern and unquailing official, it is not in human nature that he should be a popular man; so at least, has been my experience.

I have entertained some ideas on legal training for the bar and bench that are perhaps peculiar, which I will state. The difficulty of understanding the laws of England, as expounded by courts and stated by commentators, is not very great. Thus they presented themselves to my mind; but in their application to the various transactions of life lies the trouble. He who best knows how most things are usually done, is best qualified to deal with the right and wrong about which men go to law, and to apply old principles to new circumstances; and so he is the best judge of what a new statute means. To judge accurately of these, deep practical knowledge is by far more valuable than deep law learning, necessary as both are to the lawyer. He who knows mere law, but is without common sense to comprehend the facts to which his law may be applied, is a sheer pedant in his profession; and therefore it is, that we so often find a walking index of a lawyer not equal, as a judge, to a vigorous county court magistrate who never read a lawbook. But force a young lawyer to battle his way up on the circuit; to go and see the land surveyed, and the corner trees blocked before he tries his ejectment; to go into the workshop, or steamboat, or counting-house, and see how the thing is done his client is lawing about, and he will beat a dozen of his equals in capacity, crammed with law to the throat. Many instances of the kind have I witnessed. On one occasion, when just beginning, I said to a really great advocate: "Why, Mr. G., how in the world do you intend to get along in this dreadful case of murder; you have not even a law brief prepared?" "Well," said he, "what book is Mr. Attorney-General going to rely on to prove it murder?" "Mainly on Espinasse, Bacon, and Hawkins, I think," said I. "Ah, yes," was the reply, "I'll find enough, just above or just below, for my purpose, I warrant you." And so he did; and acquitted his client, who ought, undoubtedly, to have been hanged. This was one of the very best drilled circuit lawyers I ever knew. He first studied and comprehended all the facts and motives involved in his case, and then thought over how society appreciated them; and lastly, searched for law to sustain the case his facts made. And pretty much like him were Pendleton, Marshall, Spencer and Parsons; and we have many such among us now, (a little spoiled by love of parade,) who combine that common sense rough training has taught, with a deep knowledge of law.

I insist on thorough legal training and constant study; but object, whether it comes from the bar or bench, to piles of references and figures, formidable as a treasury report, gathered from the index, and having no value in the particular case; and which parade of authorities is notoriously an address of vanity to ignorance and pedantry, that ever reminds one of two grains of wheat smothered under two bushels of chaff; such being the plain condition of the little law that is applicable. How slow we all are, in such cases, to find out how merry our brothers make themselves at our expense, is marvellous. No doubt, I have been a common sufferer, as I often deserved to be when at the bar, and especially, since I have acted as judge. The practice deserves ridicule, and gets its full share.

I could quite readily have had these few and trifling materials changed into the form of an ordinary memoir, and put in the third person, presenting an appearance (but nothing more) that some other hand than my own had done the work. This manner, however, is so stale, as to deceive nobody; certainly not my own profession; and therefore, I thought it fairer to write you a letter and risk the charge of egotism, for which I care not much; whereas, I should badly wince at a charge of having resorted to the shabby contrivance, and of an attempt to skulk behind it, if mendacity or boasting was alleged. If such thing should happen here, the critic would allow that the author stands confessed in the singular pronoun, abundantly often for all purposes of recognition and responsibility.

In conclusion, sir, permit me to say, that for several days after I received your letter, no intention existed of complying with your request; but on consulting with my brother-judge of your circuit, he insisted that the object of your magazine required a different course. To procure another to write for me, was not possible within the period limited by your letter, as no one knew much about me, short of my residence in Tennessee; and then the idea that a lawyer practising before me, and an intimate friend, should sit down and coolly and truly discuss my conduct for thirty years, and my character and capacity, could not be entertained for a moment. Such a memoir could hardly be more reliable than an epitaph, or an eulogy, over the recent dead. I therefore threw off the foregoing slight sketches, which, with my vigorous memory of past incidents, cost me not much trouble, and little time. The matter may be readable, if not instructive; nor will it indicate anything that is not true.

Most respectfully,

Your obedient servant,

J. Catron.

Washington, *Dec.* 24, 1851.

www.ingramcontent.com/pod-product-compliance
Lightning Source LLC
LaVergne TN
LVHW021423110826
845150LV00007B/2060